Educational Therapy in Clinic and Classroom

Educational Therapy in Clinic and Classroom

Edited by Muriel Barrett and Ved Varma

Whurr Publishers Ltd
London

© 1996 Whurr Publishers
First published 1996
Whurr Publishers Ltd
19B Compton Terrace, London N1 2UN, England

British Library Cataloguing-in-Publication Data
A catalogue record for this book is available from the British Library.

ISBN 1-897635-93-1

Printed and bound in the UK by Athenaeum Press Ltd, Gateshead, Tyne & Wear

Contents

Acknowledgements

We are indebted to Harry Barrett for his invaluable support, the undertaking of word processing of the manuscript and the compilation of the index.

Thank you to Margaret Walker and her staff at the Tavistock Joint Library for their continued help in answering our many queries.

We are grateful to our contributing authors for sharing their teaching and learning with us in this book:

Ani Brown
Anne Casimir
Jenny Dover
Heather Geddes
Helen High
Linda Law
Ann Lewis
Anniken Marstrander
David Shott
Margaret Stokes
Marianne Sturtridge
Judith Waterfield

Contributors

1. Educational Therapy with Children who Resist Learning – by Helen High

Helen High is a child psychotherapist. She is the Joint Organising Tutor, in London, England, for the Forum for the Advancement of Educational and Therapeutic Teaching (FAETT), of the professional training leading to the Diploma in Educational Therapy. Helen gives an example of a child with perceptual problems, linked to organic causes, and contrasts his reading difficulties with those of children who have no perceptual problems, but are emotionally resistant to learning.

2. Educational Therapy with a Latency Child – by Jenny Dover

Jenny Dover chairs the Forum for the Advancement of Educational and Therapeutic Teaching (FAETT) and is a tutor and supervisor for the training course leading to the Diploma in Educational Therapy. She is the educational therapist and clinic coordinator in a London clinic. An account of her work demonstrates the theory, techniques and principles of the practice.

3. Working with Twins in a School Setting – by Anne Casimir

Anne Casimir is an educational therapist based in inner-city schools. The main focus of Anne's work is on the painful dilemmas presented by twin boys and their relationship. The questions raised at the time of referral, by a multi-disciplinary team, as to whether the twins should be worked with as a pair or as individuals, is briefly discussed.

4. A Norwegian Perspective on Educational Therapy – by Anniken Marstrander

Anniken Marstrander is an educational therapist working in a Psychiatric Clinic for Children and Adolescents in Oslo, Norway. She focuses on communication with parents and school staff and the methods used by Norwegian educational therapists working with groups, and with individual children.

5. Working Independently and as a Member of a Team – by Anniken Marstrander

By the same author as chapter 4, this chapter considers children's emotional disturbances and the appropriate treatment; should it be undertaken by an individual professional or by a team?

6. Every Picture Tells a Story – by Judith Waterfield & Ani Brown

Judith Waterfield is Advisor for Specific Learning Needs at a University in South-west England and Course Tutor for the Plymouth, England, Educational Therapy Techniques Diploma. Ani Brown is the Head Art Therapist with an Adolescent Mental Health Service based in a hospital in South-west England. The authors consider the effect their joint intervention with an adolescent group has on the complexities of the group process. How does it foster interactive behaviour and communication skills?

7. Educational Therapy and the Classroom Teacher – by Heather Geddes

Heather Geddes is engaged in research at the Roehampton Institute, London, England. Heather's work with groups demonstrates the use of her clinical skills to enable teachers to reach a different understanding of their interaction with children and colleagues.

8. Holding on to the Unbearable – by Margaret Stokes

Margaret Stokes is a Teacher in charge at a unit for emotionally and behaviourally disturbed (EBD) primary school children. She explores the use of the educational therapy techniques and approach as a way of understanding her work with Melanie, whose primary mode of communication is abusive. Margaret's work illustrates an adult's capacity for tolerating a child's extreme anger and pain, thought to be associated with that child's experiences.

9. Working with an Eight-year-old in a School Setting – by Ann Lewis

Ann Lewis has Special Educational Needs (SEN) responsibilities in a mainstream primary school in South-west England. Ann reveals the anxiety of a boy – who was not a cause for concern in the classroom – by her application of the theory and techniques learned during her training.

10. Bringing Educational Therapy into the Classroom – by Linda Law

At the time of writing Linda Law was a classroom assistant in a primary school unit for EBD children. She enables us to understand the effect of the loss of a sibling on a six-year-old's behaviour, and gives examples of his attempts to make use of his learning with her in the classroom situation.

11. Working and Learning with a Vulnerable Adolescent – by David Shott

David Shott is the Acting Head of a school for EBD adolescents. David explains how his own learning, while interacting with an individual adolescent, helped him to reassess some previously held assumptions of adolescent behaviour in the classroom, and to reconsider interactions with colleagues.

12. Educational Therapy with a Learning-disabled Adult – by Marianne Sturtridge

Marianne Sturtridge is based in a College of Further Education in South-west England. She begins with a brief account of her work with a male student, in an attempt to demonstrate that an educational therapeutic approach is not always an appropriate one. She then focuses on her attempts to interact with Martha, who is reluctant to communicate. Marianne discusses her own problems of understanding and learning, which lead into a new level of interactive communication.

Introduction

MURIEL BARRETT AND VED VARMA

Therapists of any discipline, engaged in work with children and parents, are likely to share some ideas about their interactions. The educational therapist maintains a focus on children's learning, and also enables parents to think about how their own educational experience could be affecting that of their children. The practice of educational therapy includes some didactic teaching, otherwise children will feel cheated because it has been publicly agreed, either in family and/or school meetings, that they need help with their schoolwork. The practice also makes use of the metaphor, in stories, drawing or modelling, to enable children to express, understand and acknowledge their feelings about the skills they have 'lost'.

In the first six chapters we follow the work of educational therapists who are qualified teachers, some of whom became educational psychologists, and/or psychotherapists. Their additional professional training in educational therapy includes being members of multi-disciplinary teams and undertaking personal therapy. They may work with an individual child or adult, with small groups, or with families, although the last group is not covered in any detail in these chapters. The work includes liaison with schools and other agencies who are concerned with the children referred to them. The sessions (to differentiate the time offered from lessons) are for an hour, once or twice weekly, making educational therapy a cost-effective intervention. Some educational therapists take on the role of team coordinators; many are involved in training. These chapters demonstrate the authors' teaching and therapeutic skills, and their deep understanding of the interactive process.

The two parts of the book are linked by chapter 7 – written by an educational therapist who shares her thinking with teachers – which introduces the application of a therapeutic approach to classroom teaching. This leads into the second part where the authors are mainstream or specialist teachers, except for one, who is a classroom assistant. They have all undertaken a diploma course focusing on the techniques of educational therapy with an introduction to some theory and practice.

They are not members of multi-disciplinary teams, nor have they undertaken personal therapy. Their work with families is on an informal basis whenever the need arises. (Links with other agencies are limited, although there is some contact with individual educational psychologists and social workers.) Sensitive and honest accounts of each teacher's own learning, while working with an individual, enabled them to reassess some of their previously held assumptions about classroom behaviour and to value theoretical concepts as a way to understanding their interactions with children and colleagues.

Part One

The Practice of Educational Therapy in Various Settings

Chapter 1
Working with Children
who Resist Learning

HELEN HIGH

There is a very striking difference between the child who has intellectual or perceptual problems which interfere with learning, but is not emotionally resistant, and the child who has no such handicapping problem but is resistant to learning. In many instances children show a mixture of the two. After all, most people tend to avoid tasks and activities they find particularly hard. It is not then surprising that children resist the attempts of adults to impose such tasks on them. These mixed difficulties occur in varying proportions, but it can be useful to look at 'pure' examples at either end of the scale.

Educational therapy was developed specifically to meet the needs of children whose response to specialised teaching was not commensurate with their ability. Some of these children made very slow progress while others made none.

The two pioneers of educational therapy, Irene Caspari in London and Anne-Marit Sletten Duve in Oslo, developed their work quite independently. Both set out to observe and study children's attitudes and reactions to school-like tasks and expectations. In the process they encountered children who showed marked emotional resistance to learning. Working within a clinical setting, both found that, given the opportunity and encouragement to express their feelings and fantasies, these children revealed anxieties that were inhibiting their learning. Both workers came to the conclusion that the resistance was not deliberate awkwardness. It seemed, rather, to be a way of avoiding situations where their emotions felt too overwhelming, aroused too much conflict, or were too painful or too dangerous to think about.

To highlight the difference between the child with a cognitive or perceptual problem and the emotionally resistant child, I shall give contrasting examples. The first is of a non-resistant child with a slight organic handicap and a reading difficulty.

3

Richard: a Seven-year-old with a Mild Handicap

While I was working as an educational psychologist, Richard was referred to me by his infants school (primary school for 5–7 year olds), as his teachers were concerned that he was making very slow progress in learning to read and write. He was seven years old and soon due for transfer to junior school. In assessing his abilities I found there was a marked discrepancy between his level of attainment in verbal tasks, compared with the non-verbal, while his general intelligence was on the low side of average. In verbal question-and-answer type tasks, he was consistently better than in tasks involving visual discrimination and hand–eye coordination, such as copying shapes or filling in the missing part in a drawing of a man. He also had a slight squint and his speech was somewhat slurred and indistinct.

This pattern of specific difficulty in certain non-verbal tasks, coupled with a number of signs of physical incoordination, pointed to an organic, neurological factor underlying the minor physical difficulties and the learning problems. This was later confirmed by a neurologist's report to the effect that Richard was suffering from *minimal cerebral dysfunction*. This means that, for whatever reason, either slight brain damage or a slight constitutional abnormality, Richard's brain was not functioning quite normally in some respects.

Richard attended a local education authority Remedial Centre on a full-time basis, until he reached the secondary school age of 11 years.(This was before the development of current policies which enhanced the provision for children with special needs within mainstream schools.) His progress had been very slow, but at this stage it was reviewed to consider his gradual reintegration into mainstream school.

As part of this review I re-tested Richard's reading, an experience I shall never forget. It was quite a revelation. I made a point of giving him one test in which he was reading in context and another in which he read isolated words and there were no contextual clues. (While the former gives the better picture of how a child reads in a normal, everyday context, I find the latter important in assessing how they can cope when tackling unknown words which cannot be deduced from the context.) The way Richard tackled the isolated words was impressive and brought home to me, with striking clarity, the quality of a child's struggle to overcome a handicapping condition. In the word test he really pushed himself when he came to words he found difficult. He struggled to build up unfamiliar words from their sounds, but would realise when his attempt did not make sense, say 'No' and try again determinedly until he was satisfied with his attempt. If necessary, he tried again and again and again. He persevered long after most people would have given up. He was determined to read the word correctly if he possibly could, and sometimes did so on the third or fourth attempt; on one occasion on the fifth.

Richard had obviously responded to the skilled remedial teaching he had received and there was no sign of emotional resistance to learning here; quite the opposite. It was, however, possible to see this boy struggling to overcome a handicap which was making the task technically difficult for him. He appeared to derive some satisfaction from the partial mastery of his difficulty through the persistence which enabled him to correct a good many of his own errors. How different the child who has difficulties in reading, but has no apparent cognitive or perceptual handicap, who gives up very quickly when faced with a difficulty, puts a lot of energy into avoiding reading and fails to learn, retain or consistently apply reading skills, of which he is clearly capable.

I have given this example of a non-resistant child with a slight organic handicap as a basis for comparison with those who are resistant to learning. The following examples of children with difficulties in reading and/or writing illustrate the exploration of emotional factors underlying resistance to learning and pinpoint some of the factors commonly encountered.

Peter: Intolerance of Error and Overwhelming Anxiety

Peter, who was referred to me at the age of nine as an almost complete non-reader, became very anxious when attempting to read, especially when a book was put in front of him. He was of average intelligence with no evidence of any specific cognitive or perceptual problem. I saw him once a week for educational therapy for a period of about two years.

I regularly started Peter's sessions by presenting him with a reading task. At first his anxiety would mount within minutes of starting to read and after about five minutes the anxiety felt intolerable. This was particularly so when he was reading from a book.

Success in easy stages – failure in small doses

I was able to reduce the intensity of his anxiety by avoiding the use of books altogether for a period of time. Instead, I presented reading tasks to him in small, easy stages, initially using picture-and-word matching sets involving three-letter words, with only nine words in each set. I limited the reading in the sessions to matching one set of these cards, which we repeated each week, until he achieved complete success in the task.

This way of presenting the task in very small easy stages addresses the child's anxiety about failure and is particularly pertinent for children with a long history of failure, who may no longer believe in their capacity to make progress and tend to give up very quickly if they see they are failing. Facing them with one small step at a time makes learning seem less of a daunting task and success in one step encourages them to think they may succeed in the next.

Peter was so thrilled the first time he completed the first word-and-picture matching set without a single mistake that he immediately repeated the task over and over again as if to have his fill of this new experience. I am sure it was the first time he had ever finished a reading task without making a mistake. This small success convinced him that he could learn to read and made a tremendous difference to his motivation from that point onwards.

This did not mean, however, that all signs of his resistance had disappeared. There were other and more complex factors involved in Peter's resistance to learning. I discovered that very slight and subtle variations in the way I presented new information made a crucial difference to the way Peter responded. This was only discernible through careful and detailed observation, including taking a mental note of the exact words I used when trying to help him correct his mistakes and being aware of his reactions to my words.

I used Peter's increased motivation to read from books by letting him set the pace himself, hearing him read and offering help only when he got stuck. In particular, I supplied the phonic knowledge he lacked at the precise point when he needed it. I had established by this time that he had the skill to build words from their sounds, but lacked knowledge of the sounds, so this was an area in which he needed help.

Adapting the presentation of the learning – a feeding process?

I noticed that if I made the slightest negative statement about a mistake he made, for example if I said, 'No', or, 'That word's wrong', he would repeat the mistake in the word whenever it cropped up later in that session. He persistently resisted my attempts to teach him how to read that particular word for the rest of the session. I discovered, however, by trial and error, that if I adapted the way I alluded to his mistakes, by intervening in a way that enabled him to correct himself without my telling him outright that he had been wrong, he responded very differently and without resistance. If, for instance, I said, 'Try that word again', or if he read the word 'rain' as 'ran' and I pointed to the word saying, 'Look, the letters "ai" together in that word sound "A"', he was very receptive, and usually able to correct his mistake. He also retained the information and applied it aptly to other words, not only for the rest of the session but subsequently. He could take correction, it seemed, as long as he felt he was being empowered to find the right answer rather than have his faults criticised.

This kind of detailed observation of the interaction between child, educational therapist and task, including one's own part in the interaction, is one of the educational therapist's essential tools. It helps one to understand the child's emotional reactions in the learning–teaching relationship. The understanding developed in this way can then be used to adapt the presentation of the learning material to the child's emotional needs.

Caspari (1974), in describing her work with children, compared teaching to feeding. The teacher (or educational therapist) is offering the child(ren) food for the mind, as it were, something to take in for the nourishment of the mind. Similarly, the infant or young child is offered milk, and later solid food, by the mother, for the nourishment of the body. Caspari made the point that if the infant is offered the wrong food, or the right food at the wrong stage, or if it is presented in the wrong way, the infant will not take it. She compared the educational therapist's task with the resistant child to the mother with an infant who is refusing to feed. The mother needs to find out how to present the food in a way that will enable the infant to take it in. Applying the feeding analogy to Peter, one could compare him to an infant who was unusually sensitive or faddy about the way he was fed and refused food unless the mother adapted to his need to be fed in a particular way.

Expression work

Following a learning task, part of each session with Peter was given over to expression work. Initially, his anxiety about reading was so acute, and escalated so quickly when he was engaged in reading, that I stopped him reading at the point in any session when he had clearly become too anxious to continue the task productively. At these times it seemed his emotional state was so overwhelming it was just impossible for him to cope. I then changed the activity to one which lent itself to self expression. We use the term 'expression work' to describe this deliberate use, in educational therapy, of an activity which invites self-expression. This can be done in the form of a set task, for example asking the child to draw a picture, make a model, or make up a story, or by allowing them to decide on their own way of expressing themselves through drawing, modelling, or playing with materials provided for the purpose.

In the early stages of his educational therapy, Peter's typical response, when given the opportunity for free expression at the point of acute anxiety, was to make paper aeroplanes and scribble on them in black or red. He then flew them around the room in a frenzied fashion, with accompanying sound effects, saying they were crashing and burning. He repeated this type of play, session after session, for many weeks. It expressed a repeated theme in fantasy of something very dangerous happening which ended in disaster and destruction. This fantasy and the feelings related to it seemed to be aroused by the activity of reading, so it seemed that reading had become associated in his mind with these dangerous feelings and fantasies and therefore made him anxious.

My response to his activities was receptive and attentive in a laid-back kind of way. I did not attempt to interpret the content of the fantasies in detail, and he gave very little detail in elaboration, but I did interpret that I thought he was showing me some very angry feelings.

Over a period of two years the content and quality of Peter's expression work gradually changed and the emphasis shifted from disaster and destruction to careful construction of models from balsa wood. He took precise measurements in order to get the details of the construction just right. He was very emphatic, when correcting a slight error in measurement, that he liked things to be exactly right. This enabled us to discuss how difficult it had been for him to bear making mistakes in his reading when he was so far behind and had made so many errors.

During this process his anxiety and his resistance both gradually lessened. By the time he reached secondary school age his resistance to reading had been overcome to the extent that he was reading for pleasure at home and could benefit from the special needs teaching available in his secondary school.

The detail of the work with Peter shows that there was more than one strand underlying his resistance to learning to read. There was an extreme sensitivity to being corrected and a passively aggressive opposition to being taught when his mistakes were pointed out. There was also acute anxiety which appeared, from the content of his expression work, to be connected with fantasies of danger and disaster likely to end in destruction. (High, 1978).

Nicholas: The Use of a Pencil – Confusion of Fantasy and Reality

Nicholas had difficulties in reading and writing. He was particularly resistant to writing and the quality of his handwriting varied markedly from one occasion to another. He was attending a clinic regularly for educational therapy. In a series of sessions he chose, for his expression work, to model in Plasticine and used a pencil in conjunction with the Plasticine in a dramatic and revealing way. He modelled a double bed on one occasion, decorating the bed cover with circular discs and completing the pattern by piercing the centre of each disc with a pencil. This was done with quite violent stabbing movements which pierced the bed right through. Anyone who happened to be in a bed lacerated in that way would undoubtedly have been lacerated too. He used the pencil in the style of a dangerous weapon.

In subsequent sessions he jabbed holes in Plasticine heads saying they had been shot; one had holes in the forehead, one in the mouth and nose. He then made a head with a face with two Dracula-like fangs and fitted them into corresponding holes in another face, illustrating a vampire-like attack on one by the other. Shortly after an interruption in the regular sessions, due to a holiday break, he quite explicitly modelled his therapist's face then jabbed a pencil into the cheek of the model, asking the therapist, 'Does that hurt?' In those sessions where he showed such aggressive fantasies in his expression work, he was more successful than usual in the reading he did immediately afterwards.

The educational therapist working with Nicholas left after a year and, as he needed further help, a second therapist took over. As I supervised both therapists, I was in a position to follow through what happened. His new therapist noticed that he had consistent difficulty in reading the words bed, pen and pencil. In this connection I could not help remembering the way he had used a pencil in a violent stabbing way in making a bed from Plasticine. I formed the hypothesis that the words bed and pencil (and pen, by association with pencil) were connected in his mind with the type of violent fantasy he had dramatised in his modelling activities.

On a later occasion the therapist was shown by the child's teacher a piece of Nicholas's written work on the topic, 'What Goodness Means to Me'. The writing was very uneven and uncoordinated. The therapist decided to ask him to write about the opposite side of his feelings and suggested in his next session that he wrote about 'What Badness Means to Me'. He was quite anxious about this task and resisted it by creating some initial diversions, but eventually was persuaded to carry it out and wrote: 'Badness is cutting someone's head off. Badness is cutting some-one's toes off. Badness is squashing someone's head.'

It was notable, however, that in executing this piece of written work his writing was unusually neat and well co-ordinated. When writing about goodness he produced bad writing, but when given permission to express bad feelings in the content of his writing he was able to produce good writing. It seems as if the bad feelings came out one way or another.

This example illustrates violent fantasies the child had associated with the use of a pencil. At times these were expressed, when he wrote with a pencil, by producing distortions in the quality of his writing.

Nicholas sought help in distinguishing between a symbolic action and the action symbolised when he checked out with the therapist whether jabbing the pencil in a plasticene model head hurt the therapist in reality. The expression work, by enabling him to test reality in this way, helped him to understand that it was safe to express his anger to his therapist in a symbolic fashion. This discovery helped him to clarify the difference between fantasy and reality and therefore to move forward in the understanding and use of symbols.

Fear of Words

In some cases the child's fantasies about the words on the page have imbued them with a dangerous, frightening or forbidden meaning. Barrows (1984) refers to a child she encountered, when she was working in an adventure playground, who was not learning to read. She tried to help him with his reading and noticed that he seemed afraid when they sat down together with his reading book.

She said, 'You feel frightened?'

He responded, 'Miss!, Katy! I'm scared! They're animals. That's a lion, that's a tiger, those sharp things are teeth.'

Barrows states: 'He looked as if he thought the words would jump off the page and bite him.' Here again we see the lack of distinction between fantasy and reality. Blanchard (1946) also refers to accounts of two cases of children equating the letter C with an open, biting mouth.

Terry: Reaction to Loss – Structured Games v. Free Expression

In working with Terry I found that, each time there was a holiday break in the continuity of the sessions, he would make more mistakes in reading than usual on return after the break. If I remarked on his making more mistakes than usual, and linked that with his feelings about my not having been available to him in the holidays, his performance immediately improved.

Terry's parents were separated and there came a stage when he spoke to me about that and recounted, with much distress, his memory of the day his mother first left home. He described himself and his brothers returning home from school and finding a letter on the table. He said he was about seven years old at the time. His older brother opened the letter and read it and burst into tears. It was to say his mother had left. He and I agreed that that letter probably had a lot to do with his not learning to read. Who wants to read if that is the sort of thing you find out when you read? It is not surprising if a child with that experience becomes resistant to reading. It seems that the separations from me over the holidays stirred up a bit of that feeling of loss and he temporarily lost some of the gain he had made in reading.

Blanchard (1946) again gave examples of children who were sometimes reminded of experiences of loss, or fear of loss, by the content of what they read. Beaumont, an educational therapist, wrote about the experience of often-unacknowledged loss on a child's learning with particular reference to the effect of a stillbirth in a family (Beaumont, 1988).

Use of Structured Games

Some children who are uncertain about the difference between fantasy and reality become alarmed, at times, by the free expression of their own fantasies. The child can get carried away to the extent that the fantasies feel so real they could get out of control. If the fantasy is of a violent or dangerous nature, the child feels as if something violent or dangerous may actually happen.

Terry showed this kind of anxiety on an occasion when he drew a picture of a naughty imp holding a knife. At first he said the imp was going to use the knife to cut an apple and then said the imp might fall and cut someone with the knife by accident. There was then a hint that the imp might do something for which he should be punished. Terry said he sometimes thought his drawings came to life. He also became very anxious about an unstructured game in which we played out a fantasy from a story he had told me about a word-eating monster.

He was much more comfortable when we moved on to the use of structured games with rules. The games became Terry's expression work. He invented games, or produced his own modified versions of commercial board games, which had aggressive themes of attacking one another's battleships, capturing one another's villages and so on. At this point, he seemed to feel safe to express aggression in games with rules, as the rules always impose limits, and I think this reassured him that he would not get carried away by free-flowing dangerous fantasies which might come to life. The structured framework and visual layout of the board game and the ritualised routine of turn-taking, throwing dice and making a move were a constant reminder of it being a game. Within that framework he could feel that dangerous impulses and fantasies were kept within bounds. At a later stage in his therapy, after he had recounted the painful memory of his mother leaving home, he was able to use expression work in a new way, through drawings, when something was troubling him which he could not convey in words (High, 1978).

Some children with emotionally based learning difficulties benefit from psychotherapy followed by educational therapy. While there is an overlap between the two ways of working, psychotherapy does not involve direct work on educational tasks, which, as can be seen in the children I have written about, are indirectly used to express fears and anxieties. Psychotherapists address feelings and fantasies directly, but these may, of course, include those associated with learning difficulty.

Molly: A Guilty Secret – Fear of Competition

Molly, a very intelligent 10-year-old girl, was receiving psychotherapy. Among other problems she had a reading difficulty. It emerged in her psychotherapy that she thought of printed letters on the page as human bodies and felt guilty about a past incident in which she and her younger brother indulged in sex play together. Putting sounds together to read a word reminded her of putting her body and her brother's together in a sexual contact. She resisted reading because she felt guilty about it, just as she did about the sex play with her brother. When these feelings and fantasies had been analysed in her psychotherapy she could disentangle them from the activity of reading. The guilt feelings were put back where they belonged.

At this point her psychotherapist referred her to me for educational therapy, mentioning an anxiety about being rivalrous and competitive as another factor inhibiting Molly's learning. She seemed to fear that if she competed successfully with her peers and learned better than them, she was being destructive to those she had beaten. As she was highly intelligent she had the potential to be more successful in learning than the majority of her age group. The fear of competing seemed to affect her feelings about growing up and entering into competition with her mother as an adult woman. Being able to read for oneself is an important step towards adult independence. This fear of competitiveness as aggressive or destructive is another factor which can lead a child to hold back or resist learning.

When I began to work with Molly I introduced competitive games into the sessions as a playful way of exploring and addressing this area of competition. We played board games, such as draughts (checkers), that involved skill rather than chance, and Molly was clever enough to be able to compete with me on fairly equal terms, so that she had a fair chance of winning without my making concessions or letting her win. She came to enjoy the competition and seemed increasingly comfortable about winning. The fact that I could enjoy her success in beating me, and was not threatened or demolished by her ability to compete on equal terms, seemed to help free her to enjoy her competitiveness. It was as if she felt she had permission to compete hard and win if she could. We played games for the first part of each session and she read to me during the latter part. I worked with her in this way for about a year, during which she made rapid progress in reading.

I wish to emphasise that I decided to use competitive games with Molly to allow her to use her intelligence to compete with me on equal terms. This addressed a specific area of emotional difficulty for her. This would not work if one introduced a game in which a child was at such a disadvantage they had not the remotest chance of winning. Deliberately losing to let a child win has a different feel to it and children often pick this up. Games can be used in a number of different ways in educational therapy (Caspari, 1974).

Comments on Use of Observation in the Learning–Teaching Relationship

To allow yourself to be taught by someone means accepting that the other person knows more, or is more skilful, and acknowledging your own relative ignorance and lack of skill. This has a painful side to it, particularly when it highlights glaring inadequacies as compared with your peers or juniors. Inability to tolerate the feelings roused by this can lead to resistance.

In Peter's case it seems he found it unbearable to be unable to get things exactly right by himself. This made it unacceptable to be told he was wrong. If he was told, I think he felt humiliated, as if I was rubbing his nose in his failure, and he resisted being taught. This intolerance of not knowing, while someone else knows better, is a major source of resistance to learning and being taught. An approach that emphasises that 'teacher knows best' often increases resistance. It can be difficult not to get into this situation, however. Peter's resistance to my teaching, making the same mistake over and over in spite of being told, often felt to me like a stubborn angry refusal to accept the help I offered. It could be quite infuriating and I felt like increasing the pressure on him at these points. It is very easy to get caught up in a stubborn battle of pressure and resistance when trying to teach a child who resists one's well-meaning efforts in this way, but to do so is counter-productive.

To get round his resistance I had to leave Peter to work out how to read new words on the basis of phonic knowledge I supplied. This was an implicit acknowledgement on my part of the skill he had acquired in blending sounds phonically, which, I think, left enough of his self-esteem intact to allow him to accept my teaching as something which empowered him.

The work I did in thinking about the interpersonal dynamic which took place between us within the learning–teaching relationship, was essential to enable me to understand what was going on and discover how to present the learning in a way that Peter could accept and take in for himself. Recognition of the pattern of interaction between the child, the educational therapist (or teacher) and the task makes it possible to modify one's part in the interaction and the presentation. These changes can in turn enable the child to modify his response and bring about a benign cycle which facilitates the child's learning in place of the vicious cycle of pressure and resistance which blocked his learning (High, 1978).

In the early stages of this process of modification the child may be able to change his response and to learn more readily within the relationship with the educational therapist, but remain as resistant as ever within the classroom situation at school. There is often a time-lag of several months, or even longer, between changes of this kind showing up in the one-to-one relationship in educational therapy and being reflected in the child's attitudes and performance in school.

Comments on the Function of Expression Work in Educational Therapy

The introduction of expression work at the precise point of resistance offers the child a vehicle to express the feelings that are blocking learning. If the child is invited to do so just at the point an anxiety has been stirred up by a learning task (or the prospect of a learning task), it can relieve the anxiety by providing an expressive release for it. The intensity of anxiety at such moments often lends a sense of urgency to the need to express and communicate the feelings and fantasies aroused. Offering the child a symbolic means to do so both serves this purpose and provides the therapist with a chance to gain some understanding of the underlying emotional problems through what is revealed in the expression work.

In educational therapy we regard the child's anxiety at the point of resistance as a sign that something in their mind is causing them distress and interfering with their performance. If children are able to make use of an alternative vehicle for the expression of anxiety, rather than the anxiety finding expression through failure to learn, they can separate out the expression of emotions from the learning task and this helps to free up the learning process. The anxiety or conflict is then detached from the learning activity, which has been acting as a hook on which to hang some insoluble emotional dilemma. This has been at the cost of the child's progress in learning which has been held back in the process. When offered somewhere else to place those anxieties and conflicts the child can feel safe enough, in many cases, to let the anxieties off the hook. The two areas – the emotional 'hang-ups' and the learning – which had become entangled with each other, can gradually be disentangled.

With the support and guidance of the educational therapist expression work can also give the child the freedom to go on exploring anxieties and conflicts relatively safely in a socially acceptable symbolic form. Educational therapists use the child's expression work as the basis for indirect communication about their feelings, attitudes and conflicts (High, 1985). The expression work, along with the educational therapist's receptive interest in it, also help children to link up their inner world of feeling and fantasy to the educational world, by leading them into symbolic ways of representation. I see expression work as a special adaptation of the kinds of activity and subject within the school curriculum, which lend themselves to self-expression through indirect and symbolic means, such as art, creative writing and drama. Within the mainstream school such subjects allow for self-expression and the communication of troublesome preoccupations or states of mind. Those who have reached a sufficiently mature state of mind can make use of these opportunities, which they may find therapeutic, but they will not need educational therapy as such.

The more specialised method of educational therapy is adapted to cater for the special needs of a minority of children and adolescents who have emotional problems which cause them to resist learning and restrict their educational development. The aim of the specialised intervention of educational therapy is to free up such children so that they can make use of the educational opportunities open to them.

Acknowledgement

I am indebted to Peter Masani and Mary Lacey for the use of their clinical material on Nicholas.

Chapter 2
Educational Therapy with a Latency Child

JENNY DOVER

In this chapter I discuss my work with a 10-year-old boy. I hope to illustrate some of the principles and practices that I feel are basic to educational therapy, some of which have been referred to in the introduction to this book.

William: a Ten-year-old Boy 'Stuck' in his Learning

William was a boy who generated enormous anxiety in professionals. When I first met him he looked physically robust (despite his asthma) with dark hair and a sullen, dazed expression. He was a non-starter in reading, passive in learning and described by his teachers as a terror in the playground, where he bullied younger children. His teachers found him difficult to engage at any level and were left feeling deskilled, useless and angry.

Extensive testing by educational psychologists revealed William to be of average intelligence with some specific difficulties associated mainly with poor long- and short-term memory and somewhat weak visual and auditory discrimination. Low arithmetic and information scores and an inability to blend sounds were noted. Despite considerable special needs help to address these difficulties, William remained 'stuck' in his learning. It seemed that something in the very nature of the learning process resonated with an internal conflict, making him incapable of using specialist teaching in school.

Educational therapy is a method of treatment devised to help children, such as William, who have entrenched learning difficulties. Implicit in my thinking as an educational therapist is the attempt to understand when and why the non-learning began and what maintains it. As a framework for my thinking I use psychoanalytic concepts drawn mainly from the works of Freud, Winnicott, Klein and Bowlby. These same concepts inform my method of addressing the learning problem.

Learning has a unique and individual meaning for every child. Because of their symbolic nature, reading and writing are often the chosen arenas for the expression of emotional conflict. In helping the child to a more conscious awareness of the ideas and fantasies associated with the learning, the child may be freed to move on.

Many children seen in educational therapy appear to develop satisfactorily and then stop learning at some point. This is often related to a recent trauma or environmental lapse. An example of this would be John, who stopped reading when he inadvertently discovered that his brother was terminally ill. This information was supposed to be secret and unknown to him. Since John equated reading with accessing information, an intolerable internal conflict resulted. When this was revealed and resolved in the therapy, his reading progress resumed. Similarly, David stopped achieving well in his school work when his father lost his job and became depressed. David's fantasies about his father's envious and rivalrous feelings inhibited his performance in the classroom.

Unlike children such as John and David, William did not appear to have suddenly lost skills or the ability to use skills already acquired. His difficulties seemed to start from the very beginning of his life.

In describing the process of the weekly, individual work with William over the two years he was in educational therapy, I hope to illustrate the way in which his earliest experiences in infancy, his insecure attachment and the need to defend against emotional pain, contributed to his learning difficulties. I shall also describe the use he made of the opportunity to express, explore and resolve these struggles.

There is a great deal of evidence in both psychoanalytic literature and in psychological research to suggest that early emotional and cognitive development are closely linked. Recently, for example, Lyn Murray, Winnicott Research Fellow at Cambridge University, has shown how babies of depressed mothers achieve less well on cognitive tasks than babies with responsive mothers. It is worth thinking briefly about some of the prerequisites for healthy emotional and cognitive development in infancy.

Winnicott (1986) describes the mother as 'good enough' when she can offer 'subtle adaptation to changing need'. She is closely attentive and attuned to her infant's signals and provides an environment which fits his or her needs. She facilitates a maturational process, which, given the right conditions, will take its course as part of a child's normal development. The infant, whose needs are met without undue intolerable frustration, gains a sense of 'magicking' up gratification, food, the mother. The child develops a sense of potency and confidence in correct anticipation of events. Each time the child signals hunger, for instance, and food appears, that child's sense of self is validated.

Initially, the mother/infant dyad operates as a unit. The infant's sense of his (or her) mother as distinct from himself – i.e. 'not me' – develops slowly and the disillusion in good weaning is gradual and tolerable. If all goes well, the infant, at this point, has internalised a reliable mother figure who continues to 'be there' for him despite being a separate person. Bowlby (1988) described such an infant as 'securely attached'.

Melanie Klein (1946) stressed that a vital aspect of this process is that the infant continues to experience a reliable, loving mother despite his angry feelings towards her. She posits that in the gap between signal of need (hunger) and gratification (breast), the infant may experience the absent mother as bad and persecuting. In his fantasy, the infant makes hostile attacks upon her. Klein believes it crucial that the infant feels his mother survives these attacks and continues to be available to him. The infant's developing sense of the good and bad mother being one and the same person lays the foundation for his acceptance of his own good, loving and his angry, hostile feelings.

Winnicott (1965) and Bion (1962a) describe the mother's capacity to think about the infant, receive his communications, bear them (whether hostile or loving) and make sense of them for the infant as 'holding' or 'containing'. She is managing the infantile anxiety and translating it for him. For example his discomfort and distress can be understood in terms of hunger or cold. A 'nameless dread' (Klein, 1931) in this way becomes thinkable and manageable by the infant. The infant who has been thus held in mind and thought about internalises this model of a thinking mind and ultimately becomes capable of self-reflection. An awareness of these processes in early learning underpinned my thinking about William's functioning.

Working with William

When I started working with him William lived alone with his mother, with whom he felt he had a very poor relationship. Significantly, she was given no facial features in his drawing of her. As a toddler William had witnessed inter-parental violence which resulted in his father leaving home when William was still very young. The family never spoke of the father thereafter and William's mother told him as he grew up that he had never known his father. During the time that we worked together, William's mother remarried and had another child. In the context of a happier marriage she was able to relate more closely to the new baby. This enabled her to shift her view of William – from bad and incapable to someone damaged who had 'missed out'. This was important in that she remained committed to William's therapy; a factor vital to the process which relied on regular, predictable sessions. Sadly, William's mother would not herself attend sessions in the clinic. Ideally, when a child is being seen in educational therapy, the parents would also be offered clinical sessions, often with a psychiatric social worker. This not only facilitates change in the family but also safeguards the child's therapy, which might otherwise be undermined by parents who may themselves be envious and deprived.

Soon after I started to work with William he was expelled from his primary school for his violent behaviour towards his peers, and sent to the local special school for children who were emotionally and behaviourally disturbed. This turned out to be a move that was of considerable benefit for William as he was helped by the containment offered by this new school. In the more structured, safer environment he was able to make use of the smaller classes tentatively to try out his emerging skills.

The weekly sessions with William lasted 50 minutes and took place in my room in a child guidance clinic. Initially William presented as flat, uncommunicative and unengaged. He sat at my table, ignoring the play and learning materials, with his body slightly averted from me. His face was expressionless and, unless I asked a question, he remained mute. His left hand held his right wrist as if to restrain himself.

He was unable to write words apart from his first name and couldn't tell me the sounds of the alphabet. The room seemed filled with despair and I experienced a strong feeling of hopelessness. I understood that these feelings conveyed in the counter-transference were an important communication about William's feelings and past experience.

It seemed that William had no expectation that I might be someone who might respond, understand his signals or manage his anxiety. Ainsworth and Wittig (1969), who studied the attachment patterns in one-year-olds, might have described William's behaviour as being like that of an 'avoidant' anxiously attached child. He was likely to have been the kind of baby who turned away from, and ignored, his mother when she returned after an absence that he may have experienced as being intolerable. Such a child in a classroom would simply fail to interact with a teacher, unlike other anxiously attached children who might display attention-seeking behaviour.

When I commented to William on the despair he seemed to be conveying and how hard it seemed for him to feel hopeful that I might teach him to read, he looked at me directly for the first time. This early demonstration of an attempt to understand the child's feelings is important in establishing a secure base for the work.

Oral communication seemed difficult for William. When pressed to speak he struggled painfully to find words to express himself and I was put in mind of his struggle for breath during his asthma attacks. He seemed to have little sense of himself as someone who had this or that attribute, preference or difficulty – or any sense of his own personal history. Bowlby (1988) felt that this lack of a narrative of his own life was an important distinguishing feature between securely and insecurely attached children. This incapacity for self-reflection also has implications for symbolic thinking since these children have been unable to step back and achieve an objective view.

William's experience of play seemed limited. He handled the toys and materials in the room in a rather concrete, tentative way and seemed unsure about how to make use of them, or of me, in the service of his imagination. Play is an important factor in learning in that it invests external objects with meaning. It increases self-awareness and helps children to get in touch with their deepest feelings. It strengthens the sense of potency and mastery over the environment. Play is also a precursor to learning to read and symbolise in so far as in play one object stands for another in the same way as a word stands for an object. Winnicott reminds us of the different stages in children's play, from solitary play in the presence of an adult through to mutual play (Winnicott, 1971). The latter assumes that the child has reached the stage where he can tolerate input of ideas from others into his own imaginative world. He also has to have sufficient trust to relinquish omnipotence and control. This is often the starting point of learning difficulties for abused children.

Winnicott (1965) felt that human nature could neither be explained in terms of interpersonal relationships nor in terms, only, of the inner, personal world. He felt that real creativity takes place where the subjective and objective worlds meet. He said that it was in the area of the overlap of the child's and the adult's play that therapy takes place. Engaging William in an interactive relationship where we would play together would be fundamental to our work.

In the work with William it was clear to me that I needed to be aware not only of what he had failed to learn so far, but also of what he had learned all too well. Among other things he had learned that adults were inconsistent in their behaviour and could not be trusted. He had learned that he was unable to determine events because his efforts to elicit responses had failed. And he had learned to distrust his own capacity to anticipate outcomes. I hoped, in the sessions, to provide him with a different experience with a trusted adult which might modify these views.

There were four parallel processes in my sessions with William:

- direct teaching;
- expression work;
- my commentary on the process;
- attention to the transference.

Before describing the ways in which William used the therapy, I would like to elaborate on these four components and to show how they relate to the conditions fundamental to early learning.

Direct teaching

This is an important part of the session in educational therapy. Teachers and therapists use their knowledge of the child to assess precisely what the child can tolerate and manage and how to present tasks and information. While maintaining a professional boundary there is a similarity to a mother who pays close attention to a child's communications and emotional state and sensitively introduces new ideas. They 'subtly adapt to changing need' (Winnicott, 1965) so that the frustration that inevitably accompanies learning is never overwhelming. Tasks are tailor-made to ensure some success, giving the child the self-validating experience of correct anticipation, often for the first time.

Expression work

Through drawings, stories, games, play and so on. the child is encouraged to express feelings and thoughts. Everything he does or says is accepted as a communication of his concerns or preoccupations. Through the metaphor these are explored, clarified and worked through. This might correspond to the mother who interprets the infant's feelings for him – giving the 'nameless dread' (Klein, 1931) (or positive feelings) words. The educational therapist, unlike a psychotherapist, rarely makes direct interpretations, but prefers to work at one remove. For instance, feelings might be explored through a character in the story. In this way the child's defences are respected so that very emotionally fragile children can cope with the therapy. An important part of the therapy is that the person who does direct teaching with the child is the same person who encourages, allows and bears the expression of feelings. In this way emotional and educational problems can be disentangled.

Commentary

Throughout the sessions the therapist comments on and reflects back to the child on his actions and communications. In this way she demonstrates her capacity to 'hold in mind' and think about the child. She encourages the child to develop a greater awareness of his motives and behaviour and a better sense of himself. This is not unlike Winnicott's concept of the mother 'mirroring' the infant (Winnicott, 1971). Ultimately the child develops a better capacity for self-reflection and making links for himself.

Transference

The therapist remains aware of the way the child relates to her and of the feelings he elicits in her. This ensures that she resists being drawn into dysfunctional modes of relating which might recreate his earlier experience. She provides a different experience of attachment behaviour for the child. Importantly, she accepts and acknowledges both the positive, loving and the hostile, negative feelings brought by the child, so that he feels that his 'true self' (Winnicott, 1965) is acceptable. Angry feelings, perceived as unacceptable, often get in the way of learning.

The early sessions with William

In our early sessions William was unable to initiate activities and responded in a limited, depressed way to my suggestions. He showed no curiosity about me or my room or the other children I might see. He was able, on request, to draw. His drawings were strikingly disconnected – bits of things floating in space bearing little relationship to each other. I talked about how he had ideas and pictures in his mind but how it seemed hard to link them up. Many of these early responses in our activities contained themes of inadequate nurture and of bullying. One story he told in response to a picture illustrates this. He said, 'There was a big egg and it broked open. The dragon came out and went to look for milk. But the people ran away from him and were frightened of his teeth.' His drawing of an expressionless snowman with useless, stumpy arms seemed to reflect his own frozen, impotent state. During this early phase I was conscious of my own difficulty in remaining a thinking, receptive adult who could hold on to some hopefulness about William's learning. I felt that I needed to resist adopting the role of a depressed mother. William seemed to expect me to behave and respond in this way.

William, initially, appeared able to learn a little in our sessions. For instance, he would, with a great deal of repetition and overlearning, manage some letter sounds and one or two sight words. When he returned the next week, however, he could remember nothing of what he had previously appeared to have learned. Even his own drawings seemed unfamiliar to him. It was as if everything that had gone in had gone straight through him and he had found it impossible during the week's separation to hold on to anything. Similarly, he was vague about the day, the month and the time. I talked to him a great deal about how hard it seemed to hold on to things and to believe that I held him in mind between sessions: also, how it seemed that he always had to go back to the beginning again at each session. At this point, I decided to offer William a second weekly session so that the gap between sessions was shorter.

Beginning again and remembering

It was interesting that William always had to return to the beginning. It seemed that his own beginnings contained a paradox. He had been told that he didn't know and hadn't known his father – a fact which contradicted his own perceptions. Bowlby in his paper 'On knowing what you're not supposed to know and feeling what you're not supposed to feel' (Bowlby, 1979) describes children who are unable to trust their own senses when their reality is denied. This may have exacerbated William's weak sense of his personal reality. It is interesting to speculate on how this experience may also have contributed to William's difficulty with number concepts. He had, after all, been told that William + mum + dad = 2. Barrett and Trevitt (1991) in their book *Attachment Behaviour and the School Child* discuss the difficulty some anxiously attached children have with the value of numbers.

William's mother had clearly used forgetting as a defence against her own painful memories of her marriage to William's father and had, in effect, instructed William to 'forget' his father and the violent scenes he had witnessed as a small child. It seemed as if the 'forgetting' had become generalised and got into the learning, so that remembering anything felt quite impossible.

A few months on, when William seemed to be gaining some sense of the continuity of the sessions, he began to let me know how hungry he was for stories. I had read the book *Angry Arthur* to William, about Arthur, whose anger was so enormous it becomes literally earth-shattering. I chose the book because I suspected that William perceived his own anger as frightening and destructive. He had certainly been unable to bring aggression into the learning arena, although his violent behaviour towards his peers continued in the playground.

William listened to the story with rapt attention, asking, repeatedly, for it for some weeks. From that time he continuously asked me to read to him. His appetite for the stories was voracious and I felt I was feeding a starving child. The analogy of food and learning was used by Caspari in her work as an educational therapist in 1974. William would sit close to me as I read. He asked no questions and made no comments on the text, although I continued to comment on the thoughts and feelings of the characters. In this way, over the period of our work together, we went through virtually my entire library. It was hard to know what personal meaning the stories held for him and I refrained from suggesting any. Winnicott warns of the danger of premature interpretation which can destroy creativity. I wondered whether experiencing life at one remove may have been the only safe way available at that point. I also felt that perhaps the stories were the beginning of a shared experience for us – a preliminary to mutual play. Certainly, being allowed to be a successful 'feeding' teacher felt important to me and it was with some relief that I felt I had finally located something that was eager and greedy in this very passive boy.

As time went by, and William allowed himself to be more expressive in his activities, it became clear that he was indeed afraid of his own hostile, angry feelings. It seemed as if he viewed aggression and potency as potentially harmful and dangerous. To some extent he may have been carrying his mother's projection about violent men. Her fearful expectations of male hostility and destructiveness may well have been expressed in her attitude to William. William's fear may also have been a facet of his early poor relationship with his mother who, he may have felt, hadn't continued to be reliable and loving in the face of his hostile attacks. It seemed very important that William's negative feelings towards me should be acknowledged and borne.

As the therapy progressed, William used expression work to reveal more of his anxieties about his destructive powers. His drawings, which were gradually becoming more integrated, showed powerful out-of-control vehicles travelling at full tilt without drivers or brakes. Later in the therapy, when William was developing some sense of making use of me as a teacher, and not as a depressed mother figure, he drew a bicycle hurtling down a hill with himself on it – but again with no brakes. This time, however, he added soft sacks to break the impact of the crash. It seemed he was becoming more aware of some outside support and I began to feel real hopefulness that he may find his own brakes in time. It was also clear that his drawings were developing a sense of narrative. Ann Alvarez (1994), in her book *Live Company*, has written about the importance of the therapist holding some hopefulness for the child while he may still be unable to do so himself.

William's anxiety about spoiling and destroying things got in the way of many activities. It felt as if taking things apart, for example jigsaws or words, was fraught with danger lest he couldn't put them together again. In a sense his immature symbolic thinking exacerbated this, as if dismantling a word like 'cat' might be like destroying the cat itself. In the light of this his difficulties with reading made sense. William failed to distinguish between the healthy aggression needed to tackle a problem, or to break down a word, and real, hurtful, violence.

It became clear that William needed to be able to express anger in a safe form. Thus most of my teaching relating to the alphabet, for instance, was done through 'safe' competitive games such as Word Bingo. In this way, aggression could be expressed which could be kept separate from the learning and safely ensconced in 'rules'. Allowing William to win gave him an important sense of power in his relationship with an adult. He could also see that I could bear losing without becoming retaliatory. As time went by, William learned his letter sounds painfully slowly and began to build up a small sight vocabulary. His drawings, now more integrated, suggested a new hopefulness. For instance, he drew a picture of a house and carefully added a garden with swings, a garage and a horse to ride. There was a new sense of an environment offering opportunities.

William demonstrated a growing capacity to remember what we had done in the previous session, and even recalled that 'we once read that book about Arthur who was angry...' His sense of time improved, he now knew where we were in the week, and had an awareness of weekends and of approaching holiday breaks. He seemed to be more oriented in space and time with the Tuesday and Thursday sessions in the clinic providing fixed central points.

Being enabled, gradually, to take things apart and reassemble them in the safety of our room, was an important part of the work. I tried to help William as he struggled with these tasks, to understand that I would make sure he managed and I also talked to him about his worries about spoiling and breaking things irrevocably. The first time he managed to reassemble a jigsaw successfully, he wanted to repeat the task over and over again. Clearly he was consolidating a new sense of control and potency. Slowly his confidence grew until we were able to graduate to cutting up words and reassembling them.

As time went by William was able to risk being more aggressive in shared play. For example, his 'squiggles' (Winnicott's shared drawings, 1971) developed teeth. During one session he expressed some of his feelings about his mother's pregnancy by turning my squiggle into a foetus and calling it 'a monster'. He began, also, to express more openly his pleasure in beating me in games, showing an animation and excitement which had been markedly absent in our earlier time together.

Expression work became an increasingly important part of our communication and William made use of it as a vehicle for conveying and exploring his experience inside, and outside, the sessions. His dictated stories reflected his ambivalence and struggle about growing up and becoming an independent learner. These stories were long and painful accounts of tremendous travails and efforts to achieve a goal – only to meet with a lack of acknowledgement by people significant to him.

For example: a boy sails across the oceans to an island in order to find his mother. First he has to build the boat. All manner of mishaps occur in the building, launching and navigation. Eventually, he gets back to the mainland, only to find that his mother has 'moved'. Huge efforts ensue to locate and reach her, involving yet more building, sailing and so on. When finally he does find her he tries to tell her about his struggle. Her response is dismissive and she says, 'Don't be silly!' It seemed that William was expressing his anxiety about being 'heard' and understood – and also about whether I would still be there when he returned after weekends or breaks.

Free play remained hard for William, but one day he agreed to use the sand tray. Marion Milner (1955) has said that children seem especially aware of the symbolic nature of sand play within a frame. William moved a small animal from the ledge and made it battle its way laboriously through the desert to the water trough. He said it was joining the bigger animals now. It was 'getting grown up'. The other little animal still on the ledge was waiting there. It wasn't ready to move. This play seemed to be an expression of William's tentative movement towards independent learning and readiness to 'take in' from the adult world.

Towards the end of our second year together I felt that William was showing increasing signs of emotional health. He began to show a jealous interest in 'the other kids what come 'ere' and to demonstrate his anger towards me after mid-term and holiday breaks. His reading was progressing slowly and he was now able to manage simple story books. He was incredibly excited about this and once, after reading a harder book, he triumphantly fashioned a Plasticine erection. William's misreadings were interesting. He frequently read 'bad' for 'dad'. Bettelheim and Zelan (1982) maintained that if the meaning behind the misreading is acknowledged, then the misreading need not recur. This seems to me to be exactly what educational therapy is about.

Although educational therapists work mainly through the metaphor, it is sometimes possible, and important, to link the children's material with their external reality. I decided to make a link for William when his stepfather went into hospital. He wrote a story about the struggle for leadership which occurs between a deputy who took over the gang and a returning boss. We were able to do some direct work around the difficulty of sharing his mother with his new stepfather. I was also able to link his list of physical ailments in the holiday break to his feelings about his missed sessions.

Although the gap in skills between himself and his peers remained considerable, William now saw himself as a reader and a learner and his self-esteem was considerably enhanced. The physical aggression towards other children diminished and his teachers experienced him as responsive and hopeful. It seems that the combination of this more appropriate school setting, the more contained atmosphere at home, and the clinic sessions, allowed William to move on and to develop as a learner.

The ending of the therapy with William required a great deal of time and sensitive preparation. Klein (1931) has said that the infant's experience of weaning lays the foundation for the ability to negotiate loss in later life. Clearly William had suffered a painfully premature exposure to 'separateness' in his earliest relationship. Our goodbye was likely to arouse echoes of those feelings. Over a period of months I talked to William about the ending, and of his sad and angry feelings. When I read him *Badger's Parting Gifts* (Varley, 1984) about Badger, who dies but leaves a comforting legacy of imparted skills and wisdom to his friends, William made the link. He said 'That's a bit like you showing me reading, ain't it?'

Some years after the therapy had ended, I encountered William and his mother travelling on a bus. While his mother told me with some pride that William would be starting at college soon, William, now a pony-tailed adolescent, blushed shyly. Resisting the temptation to ask him whether he remembered 'Angry Arthur', I wished him well.

Chapter 3
Working with Twins in a School Setting

ANNE CASIMIR

I work as an educational therapist in primary and secondary mainstream schools, with individual children. I have regular meetings with class teachers and/or other professionals if they are involved and I usually see parents at least once a term if they are agreeable.

Danny and Joe – Together or Apart?

Danny and Joe are identical twins whose disruptive behaviour and lack of educational progress were so severe that teachers doubted whether they could be educated in a mainstream school. After three years of educational therapy they were both achieving at above average level academically, and their behaviour was generally acceptable.

When I was introduced to these two sturdy, blond, eight-year-olds, I was immediately struck by their vigour and physical presence. I saw them separately in two one-hour confidential sessions each week of the school term, and gradually incorporated some joint sessions. The local education authority set out my brief as their individual support teacher, in two near-identical statements of special educational needs: 'To develop literacy skills, concentration, social skills and his ability to reflect on and communicate ideas and feelings so that he might express himself more acceptably and lessen aggressive outbursts.'

A psychological assessment indicated that both boys were of above-average intelligence, but had difficulty focusing on tasks and showed a very poor acquisition of basic skills. Joe had the 'poorer self-image and fewer skills'. The psychologist recommended that the boys be placed in separate classes and the family seek support at a local family therapy centre.

An unwieldy school file provided me with a vivid background picture. Danny and Joe had had difficulties settling into school, and in forming relationships with both adults and peers. There had been

27

endless behaviour incidents in the class and playground and a catalogue of exclusions from lunch-times, outings and school itself. The last teacher's report suggested that it might not be possible to educate the boys in mainstream schools, as they were so disruptive, both to other children and themselves. It was noted that the boys' needs, difficulties and behaviour were very alike. With such apparently intractable problems, educational therapy seemed to be a most appropriate way of working with these boys. My task would be to address the boys' learning and emotional difficulties, and explore the links between them. I would also seek to support the teachers working with them. I offered each boy, therefore, a confidential 'working space' (Barrett and Trevitt, 1991), in which structured learning tasks could be faced, and feelings expressed, reflected on and managed.

'Two nations are in thy womb' (Genesis, Ch.25, Verse 23)

Before beginning my work with Danny and Joe, I met with their teachers and their mother. I learned that few people in school knew which twin was which. Janet, their mother, said that the twins were detected late in her pregnancy and delivered by Caesarian section, Danny five minutes before Joe. Piontelli (1989), in her research using ultra-sound, describes twins before and after birth. She suggests that the relationship between the babies begins before birth in the shared space of the womb. Janet described the shock and isolation of the early months with two babies, and her partner's ambivalence. Joe was the baby who slept and fed less, and cried more. Danny, it seemed, had an easier constitution. Joe she felt was more like her, 'spilling out all over', whereas Danny was more like his father, Geoff, 'cautious and defensive'. She told me, tearfully, that she felt there had been 'many mistakes' in the early years. The boys had been to a playgroup but had not settled. They remained together when they had started school, but had needed a lot of help separating from her. When they were six-and-a-half years old, their sister, Julia, was born prematurely.

The boys, it seemed, had interchangeable clothes and beds and we acknowledged the need for making some clearer distinctions. The discussion focused on Joe as the more vulnerable twin. The La Trobe study of twins in school (1991) states how easily parents and teachers focus on the twin with more difficulties and needs, in an attempt at 'fairness', and how the other twin may be overlooked. They had attended one family therapy session, but Geoff, the father, was not keen to be involved and had suggested that in future only Gill and Joe need attend. Geoff seemed to be rather peripheral to this, his second family.

Edward Scissor-hands

Joe was in the class of an enthusiastic male probationary teacher. He seemed eager to engage with me. He had a soft, tactile, baby-like quality. In response to my invitation to draw a picture that would tell me something about himself, he drew a dramatic and primitive picture of a face, filling an irregular shape with wild features, then roughly shaded one half red and the other purple (Figure 3.1). When I commented on this 'split', Joe began a series of 'squiggles' (Winnicott, 1971), and dictated a story about 'Edward Scissor-hands', a video character who 'chopped things into two'. Joe also liked to listen to the story *Oscar got the Blame* (Ross, 1987), about a boy who is blamed for all the bad things that his imaginary friend does.

Figure 3.1 Joe's picture about himself.

Danny, who was more difficult to engage, was in the class of a very experienced teacher. He had an altogether heavier, harder feel than Joe and he remained reserved and cautious with me. His first picture was of a large mouse, carefully copied from a picture on the wall. He then folded his paper over and traced the mouse as a mirror image of the first. He shaded in the first mouse and left the second empty (Figure 3.2). He too began a series of squiggles about 'Edward Scissor-hands' who 'chopped people up'.

Danny liked to read the story *The Elephant and the Bad Baby* (Vipont and Briggs, 1971), who together steal food and create havoc until the bad baby goes home to mother and the elephant stomps off. It seemed that the boys felt that one mother or one therapist only had room in their mind for one boy. I thought they might unconciously feel themselves to be one boy who was being split in two.

Figure 3.2 Danny's 'Mouse'.

The see-saw

When the first holiday break approached, I felt gripped in a dynamic over which I had no control. As Danny became more engaged with me, Joe retreated. Joe began refusing to come and when he did, he drew 'squiggles' about a boy who daringly jumped from high towers but is saved by a swimming pool below. At the same time, in his sessions, Danny was making an obstacle course in the room, arranging the furniture so that he could just move around on it without falling into the 'pits' below. While Joe hurled himself into his 'pits', Danny narrowly avoided his 'lurking sharks and monsters'. In reality, swimming was an activity in which both boys excelled.

As the process of therapy evolved over the first year, it seemed that Danny, as his mother had first said to me, 'fed as the more contented baby'. He listened to on-going and age-appropriate stories, and learned to read from *The Minpins* (Dahl, 1971). His reading standard increased to match his age of nine years. Writing was more difficult; it took tremendous energy to get his pencil to flow as it rigidly jerked across the page. He played with a pair of scales, constantly trying to balance the pans. When he finished, he would put his eraser, marked with a 'D', in one pan and leave the other empty. Did this mean that Danny could thrive by emptying or erasing Joe? In class and around the school, he managed his behaviour – just. His teacher remarked that he was 'like a pot on the boil but he kept his lid on'.

Joe's behaviour, meanwhile, had become very challenging. He was excluded from school for biting his teacher. He frequently hurt himself, felt ill, or wanted to go home and remained uncooperative in his sessions with me. Joe began to fill my mind with his anxiety. He refused to read, displaying toddler 'I won't' tantrums. A crescendo was reached the day Joe said, 'I'm going to try something!' in a wild and omnipotent tone. He hurled himself up a pole that supported the ceiling in our therapy room. He fell and lay in a crumpled heap on the floor, sobbing. I felt he wanted me to pick him up like a baby and, when I didn't but commented that he seemed very hurt, he screamed, 'I am!' and ran out, with a look of fury for me. A primary assistant (Joe's favourite helper) intercepted him in the playground and brought him back, but when he later complained of a headache, his mother took him home.

I had a picture of Danny, the first born, as the big brother, defining and defending his independence in a rigid frame, and Joe as the 'little brother', still struggling to hold himself together. Joe seemed enmeshed with mother, dependent on Danny when she wasn't there (perhaps as his 'transitional object'?) (Winnicott, 1965), and rivalrous with Julia, his three-year-old sister.

In a meeting with Janet and Geoff, they frankly shared some of their differences. While Janet stressed that she had been educated at boarding school and college, Geoff revealed that he had been in trouble at school from a young age and left early. He was ambivalent about the value of traditional education and currently worked with disaffected teenagers on an urban farm project. Geoff did not attend the review meeting with the head teacher for Joe's statement (nor did he attend any subsequent meetings). I stressed how important it was for both boys to see the school's parents and the school working together, and, in particular, that the school's previous practice of exclusion, in which their parents had colluded, was a doubtful sanction for Joe.

The 'Baby Gro' book

As the first year of work began to draw to a close, the see-sawing dynamic tipped the other way. In the summer term, Joe's defiant, 'I won't read' turned into a more timid baby-voice saying, 'I don't want to read'. He became interested in a book he called, 'The Baby Gro book', in fact entitled, *I Don't Want to go to School* (Jungman and Axeworthy, 1987), and depicting a small child on the front cover in a sleepsuit.

He learned, independently, to read *I don't want to go to School*. It ends with the words, 'Perhaps I'll go to school after all.' In a series of 'squiggles', Joe drew the Thames Barrier and wrote: 'This is the fourth Thames Barrier. The barriers are to stop London flooding. One day the barrier broke. It got a hole in it and the water started to flow out.' His writing sprawled uncontrollably across the page. He, too, was growing and flowing.

While Joe became better, Danny was simultaneously getting into more trouble. His business-like approach to learning was foundering. His parents 'forgot' to attend the review meeting for his statement. The crucial issue for me, when working with these twins, was, could they believe that one therapist could hold them both in mind at once? To try

and steady on the see-saw, I requested an extra hour a week to work with
them together, a request supported by the school and psychologist. This
was turned down by the education authority. I did not feel the boys were
ready to forfeit any of their individual time and so this matter was left
until Danny and Joe took it into their own hands.

'Hang Man'

It was Joe's last session before the mid-term break and although I had
given him plenty of preparation in previous sessions, a fact that he had
'forgotten'. When I reminded him again, he impulsively ran out saying
that he 'must get Danny'. They both returned and asked to play a
favourite game, 'Frustration', in which landing on your opponent's place
sends him back home, that is displacing your opponent is a strategy for
winning. Joe leaned on Danny's arm as they played; Danny looked very
uncomfortable. When Joe thought he might lose, he refused to play on.
They did a 'hangman' for me to guess. It read 'Danny and Joe'. I
acknowledged this message, but as we ended the session Joe pointed
out that this had been 'his' time and he wanted to come to Danny's time
after the playtime break. 'It would be fair', he said. Danny rejected this,
despite my attempts to talk about the situation. Joe left dejected.

When I returned from coffee, I found Joe fighting with a smaller child,
outside our room, and Danny trying to intervene. On seeing me, Joe ran
outside with Danny following, trying to hold on to him, but Joe left the
premises. I informed the school office and Danny now offered to go back
to his class, looking quite defeated. Meanwhile, mother had phoned to
say that Joe had arrived home but wanted to return to school. Danny had
a curtailed and sad session before I collected Joe from the school office.

This painful episode demonstrated the complexity of the boys' relationship. Clearly they could not both feel held at once. Rivalry and envy
were intense. However, I felt that it marked the beginning of some real
shift in their relationship.

When Joe came back to school, he began to listen, take in and seek
adult guidance. He drew a series of 'squiggle' pictures showing his home
and school. In the final picture, he depicted the other members of his
family at home and then said, 'You know where I am,' putting himself in
the school. Just before the end of term, Joe broke his arm, falling out of a
tree, but he attended school and managed himself impressively. Over the
summer he enjoyed a cub-scout camp holiday despite his arm. But
Danny was now expressing more of his pain. He acknowledged that Joe,
'spoiled his time', and that he couldn't get his own 'proper place'. There
were more behaviour difficulties in class and around the school. When
Joe broke his arm, Danny was absent for the final two weeks of the
school year with diarrhoea. I had to say 'Good-bye' to him for the
summer by letter and telephone.

A painful separation

When the boys returned to school after the summer holiday, Joe was in the class of an experienced teacher. He was ready to put his energies into learning to read and write. He told me that I should see him until he went to secondary school. Danny now found himself in a class where he felt less contained and his behaviour was loud and restless. Janet reported that rivalry with little sister Julia for her attention had shifted from Joe to Danny. She let me know that Geoff was not around very much at home and she was fearful that he might leave. When she went away for a week to look after her grandparents, she took Joe and Julia with her but left Danny with Geoff.

The Pig and the Wolf

In his sessions, Danny now clearly began to use writing, which he found so difficult, as a metaphor for communicating his struggles. He made up a crossword, 'Clues about Danny', in which answers included the words 'twin', 'first', 'winner', and also 'balance', 'equal', 'learning' and 'understanding', contained in the rigid frame of the crossword box. But Danny was getting noticeably fatter; and he was expressing his anxieties more openly. We read *The Iron Man* (Hughes, 1968) together, a story which perhaps reflected both the strength and the fragility of his own defence.

Danny now began writing his own first coherent story: 'The Pig and the Wolf'. In it a wolf went into a sweet shop to buy some sweets. But the pig shopkeeper is suspicious that this is the wolf who had eaten his brother and says, 'Get of my shop or I'll call the police'. The wolf does not go and he is put in prison. Here, Danny carefully ruled the bars of the prison over the picture of the wolf. But the wolf gets out on bail and 'goes and eats the pig's mum'. 'Then the pig eats the wolf because he is so CROSS.' I commented on the murderous anger and intensity of the rivalry over the mother. Danny said this was the beginning – he had more stories to write.

The Man with Two Brains

I had difficulty in sustaining Danny's effort as he so painfully tried to put his feelings into words and ideas. He worked from rough drafts and began to produce a 'neat' folder in his own, barely legible, handwriting. On the cover Danny drew an irregular shape, which he then divided into two identical masses nestling together, one infant on top of the other and containing sharp teeth. He labelled each part like a scientific drawing as 'A Brain'. This, he explained, was a 'Siamese Brain' and he began a story called 'The Man with Two Brains' (Figure 3.3). The man in the story had an operation to separate the Siamese brains. One half of the brain was removed and put into his foot (Figure 3.4). The man was a footballer and lived in fear that his enemies would chop off his foot. Luckily, because of the brain, his foot could move away very quickly and several attempts are made to chop off the foot until finally a man does just this (Figure 3.5). A big investigation is launched to find the other brain. 'The police found the thief and the hospital sewed the foot back on. The man thought that he would lose his foot again but he didn't and the man who chopped it off got 107 years in prison.'

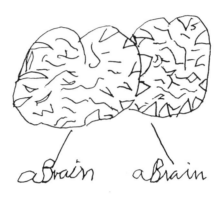

Figure 3.3 Danny's 'Siamese Brain'.

Figure 3.4 Danny's 'Man with two Brains'.

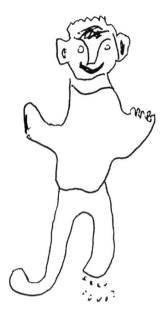

Figure 3.5 Danny's 'Man with foot chopped off'.

A sharp weapon

While Danny was struggling with his writing and his behaviour, Joe was learning to read from *Fantastic Mr Fox* (Dahl, 1970) about a 'good' thief and family man. Joe's favourite game was 'Snakes and Ladders'; in which he continually tried to cheat to win. He dictated a story about a 'very dangerous carving knife' in a butcher's shop where he, Joe, worked. One day the butcher leaves the knife on the counter while he goes out the back. 'A man came in and threw it at me. It nearly cut right through me.'

At this time Joe could be overtly affectionate, offering me small gifts he had made. One day he drew a large heart and said, 'You think this is a heart, but if you turn it the other way round it's a sharp weapon,' pointing it directly at me. So his feelings towards me could turn or tip very quickly in the opposite direction, I commented.

Joe progressed well, brought his reading up to average for his 10 years and managed his behaviour until we came to the last term of the year. He began to get into trouble again as his anxiety increased about leaving his class teacher. I was unavoidably absent for a day, and returned to hear that Joe had been in two fights, and to find him locking me out of the room. I called to Joe inside, acknowledging that he had felt shut out, and he opened the door but darted out. He refused to engage with me and, later that day, was excluded for biting his teacher.

However, during this summer term Danny had settled in his class. It emerged that although Joe was to be moving up to his final year in primary school with the same teacher he liked and had done so well with, Danny was to go into the class of the much loved cub-scout leader. Once again, they were fighting over one person.

Survival of the fittest

When we met again for our third and final year of work, the see-saw had tipped again. Danny seemed back on top of the see saw. The staff noticed how 'different' from each other the boys were becoming. Danny looked considerably heavier and grew his hair longer. He had his own set of friends. Joe plunged back into his sessions with me, talking of Siamese twins he had heard about, born during the holidays. They had had a long operation to separate them, but there was only one heart and one of the twins had died. I felt that Joe's 'wound' was oozing with envy of Danny's being with a favourite teacher. Whether he could survive either with or without Danny seemed to be at stake. The decision about secondary schools – together or apart – was now being considered. I went with both boys and their parents to look around two local schools. The boys favoured different schools, Danny preferring the ostensibly more academic and Joe the more nurturing. Their parents seemed to support this.

'Never write the enemy off'

Danny continued putting his energies into his writing and explored his desire to win with a story about 'Andrew Gold', the Olympic sprinter, the fastest in the world. Just before the race, his arm is broken by the second-fastest runner, who thinks that this will help him win. But he is wrong and Andrew Gold wins the race. He is pictured cross and spiky in his Nike running shoes. Joe, meanwhile, began a game he called 'Never Write the Enemy Off', in which he constructed an elaborate defence system of cardboard castles with look-out posts. He would arrange two enemy groups of small toy figures, but he didn't play out the action. The two boys went away for a week on a school trip. They returned to find that they had been signed up for the same secondary school – Danny's choice. Janet justified giving them an 'equal chance' and indicated that Geoff was very much in favour of this. Perhaps the complete separation felt too drastic, but Joe was mortified.

Did he fall or was he pushed?

Joe now began writing, and primitively illustrating, a large comic book that he called 'Cyclops and Little Brother'. The characters were: 'Terminator Two', drawn like loose parts of a female body, and a big and a small 'Cyclops' brothers. Terminator Two eats little brother and says, 'Yummy', and then kills big brother in a fight. She then regurgitates little brother, and then kills big brother in a fight. She then regurgitates little brother, who 'zaps', or kills, her.

In the next instalment, 'little brother, Cyclops' faces another aggressor, this time on top of a high building with a swimming pool beneath. When I commented on how worried 'little brother' must be, Joe said, 'No, the swimming pool has reinforced glass over it, he's dead.' The final picture showed a 'King' and a large 'splat' (Figure 3.6).

Figure 3.6 Joe's 'King' and 'Splat'.

Win or die

Joe, predictably, got into trouble in school and was excluded for fighting and hurting a helper with a raised chair. In his sessions 'chess' became the symbolic battle ground, in which one player gains ground by displacing the other and one in which you cannot move successfully without equally considering your partner's counter-moves. Bettelheim and Zelan (1987) describe chess as a 'war game' in which players learn to master and control their aggressiveness. In the session following Joe's fight, he said that he was going to 'murder' me at chess – it was 'win or die'. 'So there's no place for losing,' I reflected aloud.

Joe asked me if I'd heard about the boys who had murdered a toddler, James Bulger. 'They were 10 and he was only two. One of the boys said that he was the big brother.' When I wondered what might make big boys, brothers, want to murder little ones, Joe replied, 'Money! Maybe the little kid's dad had paid the boys to do it.'

'So the father wanted to kill his own son,' I reflected.

'Yeah,' Joe said, 'because the mother left him so they killed her son.'

Britton et al. (1989) draws our attention to the need for a child to progress by moving outside the Oedipal triangle. Joe, it seemed, felt threatened by the retaliatory, murderous feelings of an Oedipal rectangle in which he had clung to the illusion of himself and his mother as the couple.

A double murder

Joe went on to explore his Oedipal rivalry in the first long story he wrote in neat form, the story of rival ghosts, 'Boo and Aarhh'. Oscar is a boy who gets the blame for what a ghost called 'Boo' has done. Oscar is very angry with Boo, but Boo lives in a cave defended by an electric fence. Oscar jumps into the electric fence and dies. 'Aarhh', he says and becomes a ghost. The two ghosts are drawn side by side, foetus-like, in a womb surrounded by an electric fence (Figure 3.7).

Figure 3.7 Joe's 'Ghosts'.

'Boo doesn't like Aarhh. He feels angry and upset because his wife left him. She left him because Aarhh told her that Boo loved someone else. Really Aarhh just wanted Boo's wife to himself, so he tricked Boo.' The story continues and Boo and Aarhh fight to the death because Boo wants to get his own back. Aarhh shoots Boo and they both die. 'Boo's wife, Mrs Aarhh, comes to pay her last respects and doesn't know whether to laugh or cry.'

Again, intense rivalry over the mother/wife is evident.

The heart of the matter

Meanwhile, Danny was fortifying his defences reflected in a well-written story, 'The Castle'.

'Once upon a time in Scotland there was a castle. It was always under attack. The castle belonged to King George but he had an enemy, his great cousin, the Duke. He said that the castle belonged to him.' Danny's picture of the castle spread across a double page with exactly half on each side, the breast-like doorway straddling the two. One half was drawn in black and the other in grey, each flying a flag, the colours in reverse.

'Now the Duke was planning an attack, so the King put up his defences. The King was in a stronger position, as the Duke had to ride up the hill and he was defeated. Now the Duke wanted to retaliate but the King saw him coming. They went into hand-to-hand battle, but the King chopped off the Duke's hand and took his dagger and threw it at the Duke. It hit him in the heart.' The rivalry seemed so intense that at a deep level Danny felt the need to 'kill off' his brother.

A balancing act

In our last term, all three of us now felt ready to work together. We agreed to use the first session each week for individual time and the second for an hour-and-a-half together. Joe agreed but Danny added a proviso that he would only stay for one hour: 'That was all he needed.'

The term began with the final review meetings for the boys' statements. Danny's was scheduled first. It was noted that this was the first year that both boys were achieving well, although Danny was 'ahead'.

Danny was described as 'achieving at an above-average level across most areas of the curriculum'. He had been placed third in his class on the London Reading Test and 'behaviour incidents had dropped from three per week to three per year'. Janet was pleased and described Danny as 'more like her, more reliable'. A week later, she missed Joe's review meeting, being confused about the times. Joe's review was also positive, but recognized that he remained more vulnerable. This was reflected when the local education authority awarded an extra hour of support per week for Joe, to commence at secondary school.

The treasure chest

Our joint sessions were to be every bit as challenging as I had expected. Joe sat facing me, demanding eye contact. Danny sat at the end of the rectangular table, next to me and nearer the door. I read *Herbert and Harry* (Allen, 1986) with them. In this story, two brothers go out fishing and find a treasure chest. As they fight over the treasure, Herbert pushes Harry out of the boat and takes the treasure to a mountain, where he defends himself in an armed fortress, while Harry swims to safety. At the end of the book, they are pictured as old men – Herbert still defending himself on the mountainside and unable to sleep, while Harry, surrounded by family, sleeps soundly. This story contained the rivalry, envy and guilt that had ensnared Danny and Joe. Both boys declared, 'I want to be Harry!'

The Story of Two Brothers

Now Danny and Joe were ready to write their own 'Two Brothers' stories together, with me. We took turns to write: I began, 'Once upon a time there were two brothers who were both kings.' Joe added, 'They fought all the time over who would rule the biggest state in the biggest country.' Danny contributed, 'Once they had the biggest battle you have ever seen: blood, livers, guts, flying everywhere.' I continued, 'There seemed no way this battle could end.' Joe added, 'But one of the brothers who . . .' Danny dived in, continuing, '(who)se name was Joe of Canterbury . . .', and Joe completed the story with, '. . . got shot in the heart and died.' I wondered, aloud, whether the other brother would survive his guilt.

Just before our next joint session, Danny was involved in a fight. Joe arrived first as usual. Danny remained slumped outside the door, red faced and thunderous. Joe and I expressed our feelings of missing him and eventually he joined us. Danny half-sat on his chair and began to write messily in our book. Joe accused him of spoiling it and began taunting him. I suggested Danny's writing was fine when it was in fact a mess. Danny laid into Joe, thumping his back, as Joe turned away and buried his head in his hands. Danny collapsed back into the soft chair, head bent down, and began sobbing. They looked like broken book-ends. After a while, I commented that Danny wanted to put his upset feelings into Joe. Joe now sat up and said that he was all right. Danny stormed out. I felt split in two, obliged to stay in the therapy room but worried about Danny's welfare.

Joe seemed lifeless as we played cards and he couldn't keep to the rules. He had pushed Danny out but also needed him there as a container (Bion, 1962a). Joe suggested that I try and get Danny back, throwing a bean bag at the empty chair. I called Danny back and he picked up the bean bag and threw it at Joe as he sat down and looked affectionately at me. Joe threw the bag back at Danny. I suggested, anxiously, that we should begin our next story and wrote, 'Once there was a king . . .'. Danny was rotating his arms in opposite directions. I said that I felt pulled in opposite directions. I wanted to give them both attention, but they were making it very difficult for me. Danny sat down and continued the story, '. . . who lived in the north of the kingdom.' Joe now wrote, 'He had a brother who lived in the west.' Danny added, 'He was his brother's worst enemy.' Joe now continued, 'One day King Danny's castle was hit by a tornado.' Danny drew the castle on top of a hill, breast-like, and Joe added in the tornado. Joe wrote on: 'King Danny's castle was in ruins so he pleaded with King Joe to help him.' Danny was getting edgy and wrote: 'King Joe said thank you for asking.' Each drew himself, King Danny cross and frowning, King Joe smiling vacuously (Figure 3.8). Despite the deep rivalry, a basis for cooperation appears to be depicted.

Figure 3.8 'King Danny' and 'King Joe'.

My brother's keeper?

The intensity of the work being undertaken stirred some further behavioural difficulties. The afternoon that I was due to meet Janet to discuss Joe's 'forgotten' review meeting, there was an explosion in the dining hall. As I was talking to Janet, the head teacher came to my room with both boys. It transpired that Joe had been in a fight with a boy who was 'cussing his mum' and Danny had dived in to help Joe out, threatening the boy with his dad. Joe hurled a chair and a helper was hurt. Neither of the twins had responded to calls to stop and they were now both excluded from school for five days. For Danny this was the first exclusion in three years. Rage and despair filled the room. Joe stood in the corner with his back turned; Danny slumped in a heap on the floor, shoulders hunched and shamefaced. Janet was close to tears.

After some moments, I found the energy to reflect aloud how disappointed we were all feeling, when there had been so much hope – too much perhaps. I also linked the 'explosion' with Joe's disappointment that his parents had missed the review meeting for him. Joe, seemingly relieved that his feelings had been acknowledged, suggested that we all play cards together and the mood lightened, but when he started winning Danny furiously refused to stay in the room. Janet followed him out.

I thought that Danny felt quite betrayed by me. I had encouraged him to work together with Joe, to include him and now he was mortified. Joe clung on to his time with me, but was lifeless and foundering. I dreamed that Danny brought a knife to the next session: it was to attack *me*, I realised, representing his mother in the transference.

When the boys returned from their exclusion, I read the story of 'Esau and Jacob' with them. The atmosphere was electric. I felt that I had their attention simultaneously for the first time. As it became clear that Jacob and his mother deceive the father and cheat Esau, Joe became restless. When Jacob has to flee for fear that Esau will kill him, Danny became equally uneasy. At the end, when there was some reconciliation between Jacob and Esau, Joe commented, 'There should never have been a blessing on the first-born.' Danny added, 'The parents shouldn't have had favourites.' Joe then asked, 'Why didn't Esau kill Jacob?' and Danny answered, 'Because it wasn't really his fault.' They had begun to obtain some insight into family complexities for twins – including a feeling that brotherly cooperation was possible.

Old Men

Now they came to write their third, and last, brothers' story which they called 'Old Men'. They wrote together, as a duet: 'Now both brothers are old men. They worked hard for many years ruling their kingdoms. They had many children they loved very much. They had many disappointing battles. Now they are in their nineties and ready to die. They are going to die of gangrene from all the wounds they got in their battles. They have two granddaughters who are twins. They are eight years old and getting on fine.'

This story was so moving that I felt no futher comment was needed. When both then picked up packs of playing cards and began quarrelling about which pack to use, I suggested that we play with both packs together. As we were playing together, I realised that no one was keeping a score – winning and losing were both possible, it was no longer win or die.

Danny left the session early, as usual, and Joe stayed. As we played chess, Joe remarked that he didn't cheat any more. 'No?' I prompted.

'I don't really have to,' he said.

Teamwork

In their last individual sessions, Danny wrote a poignant story of 'Lenny and Paul', a bobsleigh team, driver and brakeman, who are entering the Olympics together for the first time. Despite Paul breaking his foot they win. The final picture showed a single gold medal, hanging on a ribbon that 'one of Lenny or Paul won'.

Joe, meanwhile, was writing poems: 'Violent Man' who drives a van. In a second poem he wrote, 'Cake and Chocolate'. He said both are good to eat, 'But chocolate cake is very rich, in fact too rich to eat'. His illustration shows one candle on a breast-like cake.

In our final meeting together, we read *Amos and Boris* (Steig, 1972) about a mouse and a whale who save one another's life and develop an intimate friendship 'sharing everything', but eventually have to part. The story reflected the boys' relationship with each other, and their separation, as well as some aspects of their relationship with me.

As a final gesture each boy drew something to remember our work by. Joe drew two identical flags, touching each other, on a single shaft but coloured their three stripes in reverse colours. Danny drew a box with two crossing pathways through a maze, calling it 'Land of Traps'. I thought that Joe's picture was an external symbol of the boys' relationship from a common origin, while Danny's was a symbol of the inner complexity of their relationship. Joe commented that Danny's picture looked like an assault course. Danny's eyes lit up as he invited Joe to help him make an obstacle course with the furniture, as he had done in his early sessions. The boys went together, Danny first then Joe, holding hands over the dangerous pits.

Conclusion

In working with Danny and Joe, I learned how difficult it can be for twins to thrive simultaneously. In their jostling for position it became clear, in the transference, that these boys could not both feel held in mind at once. In the absence of maternal containment, they tried to evacuate bad experiences into each other by projective identification (Klein, 1946). This influenced their inability to hold on to, and digest, experience; they behaved impulsively. While Joe remained less separate from his mother, he lagged behind Danny in his development. The precarious Oedipal rectangle was constantly undermined by the more manageable triangle which excluded their father.

The boys gradually separated and developed their individual wholeness as they projected their feelings on to a therapist. As they became more able to digest and think about their experiences, their behaviour changed. They became able to symbolise and express their ideas and feelings in the metaphor of story writing. Their academic progress rapidly increased, reflecting their abilities and has continued, since the end of the process of educational therapy, along with their social skills. Both their report cards, after a year at secondary school, showed several A and B grades, and their behaviour was reported not to be problematic.

Chapter 4
A Norwegian Perspective on Educational Therapy

ANNIKEN MARSTRANDER

An Outline of My Understanding of Educational Therapy

As a bold initiative in Oslo in 1953 the newly founded Nic Waal's Institute of Child and Adolescent Psychiatry appointed Norway's first educationalist to work in such an establishment. Extended vocational training for pre-school and primary school teachers began in 1958 and a report in 1990 led to the legal requirement that every polyclinic for children and adolescents should have an educational therapist on its staff. Ongoing efforts are being made to establish much-needed training places in all these clinics.

Nic Waal's Institute has three main tasks: education, research and clinical work. The principal education task is to train educational therapists, but it also runs postgraduate training programmes for doctors, psychologists and social workers. In common with similar clinics in Oslo, it has responsibility for a region of Oslo, i.e., there is close contact with the schools, the child welfare department, the kindergartens, and municipal (community) health clinics of the region. In Norway we call these clinics 'psychiatric polyclinics for children and juveniles'. In addition to the educational therapists, the staffs of the clinics include psychiatrists, social workers and psychologists. I might also add that the term 'polyclinic' is used in Norway for any clinic where a referral must come from a medical doctor (a GP) in order to be accepted for any treatment.

Training Teachers to Become Educational Therapists

Our basic teacher-training helps us to understand that children, like plants, require space and care to develop their own individuality, with the aim of providing a suitable environment which will enable them to do so. Educational therapy in Norway goes further, in that it is based on a psychodynamic model so that therapists focus to a greater extent on innate abilities and feelings. We aim to arouse latent key abilities, while allowing the children to express appropriate emotional reactions to learning. We hope they will become aware of their positive abilities and know that their feelings are part of themselves. For some children the discovery of this 'new' part of themselves, i.e., their feelings, may become the basis for a future, more positive self, providing the impetus for new learning coincidental with the development of the ego. Many children and adolescents referred for therapy have experienced psychological pain and require empathy to reduce their resistance to learning, and it is essential for them to feel that they are being understood.

Individual treatment by an educational therapist may not be sufficient to initiate changes in a child's intra-psychic structure related to learning. While working with the child the therapist must bear in mind the nature of the child's circumstances at home, at school or in the kindergarten. In these environments the child may experience loss of skills and show weak ego-functions and it is our task to consider how we may modify the child's perception of these surroundings which are sometimes negative.

Teamwork: the therapeutic alliance

The therapeutic alliance describes our policy of aiming to establish and maintain contact with those, such as parents and teachers, who are in long-term contact with the child or adolescent. This is not easily achieved if the primary carers are dismayed by the major behavioural disorders they encounter in their child. Any teacher, too, has a right to feel frustrated when classwork is disrupted by pupils who seem unable to cope with their own feelings. I believe that the essential element in establishing this alliance is that the therapist empathises with the child's, the parents' and the teacher's situation. (This is discussed in more detail in Chapter 5.)

Types of Emotional Disturbances Dealt with by Educational Therapists

The child's ego function (attitude) is revealed through manifest behaviour such as speech, mimicry, play, movement, restlessness/calmness and so on. A referred child may display poor linguistic development, make facial expressions without mimicry, have a poor contact function (a reluctance to interact with others), be limited in play, and be either passive or over-active towards the immediate environment. Problems underlying the referrals may be such matters as refugee or immigration difficulties, divorce, physical and/or sexual abuse, bereavement, domestic violence, suicide attempts, bulimia, anorexia, encopresia and enuresia. Any likely physical disorders will already have been assessed prior to the referral. Obviously, many cases referred to a clinic will not require the involvement of an educational therapist but others may be so unambiguous that a member of that discipline will be given responsibility at the initial stages of treatment. Some referrals give detailed accounts of the behavioural disorders displayed at kindergarten or school, and these will be the educational therapist's responsibility, but others may briefly outline difficulties at home or outside it. These latter cases will become the responsibility of other specialists but there are cases when the educational therapist may make a valid contribution at some later stage. I will give two brief examples:

- **Nina: an anxious six-year-old**

    Nina, a six-year-old girl, came to the polyclinic showing great anxiety. The psychologist worked for six months, with her and the family, before the educational therapist began work on her learning blockage. After nine months her drawings became more skilful, more colourful and more detailed, and her capacity for play returned.

- **Omar: an eight-year-old boy with language difficulties**

    Omar, an eight-year-old immigrant boy, was referred to the clinic because of language difficulties and loneliness. He could not speak Norwegian. Several conversations with the family gave the boy motivation to learn; also, the educational therapist helped him to master the language and enjoy school subjects, which in turn helped him to take part in the social life with his peers.

Most of the young people referred to us have, at some point, failed to move into adolescence, or to establish good interpersonal relationships, often as the result of over- or under-stimulation during their earlier learning. Research has clearly shown how important are the interactions between the primary carer, the child, and the environment, in providing opportunities for varied and rich experiences that further the child's cognitive development. The children of mothers who give them love and care, talk to them, do not use physical punishment, encourage positive experiences, and are sensitive to their needs and wishes, are able to develop independence, a high degree of competence and normal cognitive abilities independent of their cultural background (Rye, 1993).

The strain that the child is subject to during adolescence may inhibit linguistic, motor and cognitive skills and will affect the ability to function socially and emotionally. A child referred because of severe behavioural disorders out of school is likely to display these intra-psychic weaknesses in the classroom. 'It is when conditions during children's adolescence form an early and ongoing negative development that early intervention may have a particularly positive effect on their development. The purpose of early psychosocial intervention is to strengthen, enrich and expand the positive experiences of children's interaction with caregivers (Rye, 1993). Special education therapeutic theory stresses this view as being imperative for the child's development.

When behavioural disorders are centred on the home the psycho-dynamic understanding of the educational therapist can make a valid contribution to the early intervention. Our expertise may enable the parents to be aware of positive factors and not 'just' the negative ones in their child's behaviour, and thus improve the interaction within the family.

Parents may deny that their child has a behavioural problem and then we are faced with the dilemma of presenting an issue which, for the parents, does not exist. Daniel Stern's approach is to pose the question, 'How can an educational therapist along with the child/adolescent and parents take part in each other's subjective experiences?' Stern focuses on the question of sharing, or of having in common, emotional states, and how to get inside other people's subjective experiences and then let them know that you have arrived there, without using words (Stern, 1985).

Stern's theory alerts us to the importance of interaction but warns us that it is not achieved overnight. When undertaking preventive work we have to decide whether it is advisable to convey to the parents the view that incipient traits may become manifest. Is it right to suggest the existence of problems that they are not aware of? Anna Freud points out that children do not show a very regular pattern in their growth – thus problems may change or even disappear (Freud, 1965).

There are other cases where, at the outset, the educational therapist seems to have no relevance. A constipated child is an obvious case for a physician; a psychologist, a social-worker or a psychiatrist, may start by focusing on the home environment and family interaction. Factors outside the home may also have some relevance and here the educational therapist's contribution of observing a child at school may reveal other positive or negative elements. Psychologists and psychiatrists are also likely to consult teachers when considering their patients but that does not necessarily exclude the educational therapist from their deliberations. Educational therapists are involved in looking for and studying the influences that the child is subjected to when positive behaviour is demonstrated and, conversely, what prompts negative responses. These are important observations which will later enable the therapist to build up the child's functional competence. 'Findings of deviations (negative behaviour) may assume such predominance that they become destructive to already existing resourceful ego-functions (positive behaviour).

Findings of resources are instrumental in strengthening the ego' (Marstrander 1991).

When an educational therapist is to be involved in the treatment of a referred child the expertise of the educationalist with child-psychiatry training may provide much of the help that the child needs. In developing this expertise educational therapists, in common with the other disciplines, have become increasingly aware of the need to pay greater attention to the mother/infant interaction. In observing this relationship one can see the potential for a child's social, emotional and cognitive development. This mutual contact gives the infant a feeling of security but where the mother, or other caregiver, is uncertain of her influence it may be wise to consider the advice of a psychologist. Henning Rye suggests:

- Encouraging the mother through emphasising that what *she* considers to be good for the baby *is* good for the baby.
- Demonstrating to the mother, if she is inexperienced, what she can do together with the child to achieve contact and intimacy.
- Making the mother aware of the fact that the child does have his or her own initiative, needs and wishes.
- Stressing that the child reacts positively to what the mother is doing when she responds to the child's own signals (Rye, 1993).

From Referral to Team Diagnosis

All referrals to the Child and Adolescents Psychiatry Clinics are assessed by a medical doctor. At the clinic a team decides which disciplines are to be involved with the case; then it is likely that the next stage will probably be to make contact with the parents or other primary carers. Teamwork is important here in order to establish the role, if any, of the educational staff in relation to the likely involvement of social workers, psychologists and child psychiatrists.

The first meeting with the parents aims to establish a rapport which will enable the team to help the child in cooperation with the parents. While the therapists may be considering the parents' interaction they, in turn, will be assessing the therapists. The mutual endeavour of both parties should be to establish 'a secure base' (Bowlby, 1988) between therapists and parents to ensure the quality of the work. Subsequently the therapists would wish to see parents and child together to provide some insight into their functioning as a family (or part of it): for example, to discover how they respond to each other's stimuli, the extent of dialogue between them and what signals they send to each other.

Younger children are more at ease when these meetings take place in familiar surroundings, such as a playroom, and being able to arrange a setting based initially on the child's needs may have positive effects on the interaction between parents and child. Some adults may find the play setting a threatening one in that they have to relate to the child and respond to their needs. How do the parents see their respective roles in this situation? And what about the child's demeanour, ability to play, posture, language, etc?

How do adolescents react to a first meeting with the polyclinic team?

'Adolescents with psychological problems generally have a low self-acceptance' (Ystgaard, 1993). For adolescents it is essential to provide a venue where they will feel accepted and respected. The therapist must be cautious in approach to these vulnerable young people who, among other things, consider themselves losers in the eyes of adults.

After the initial meeting the therapists assess whether there is sufficient information to determine a course of treatment. Will it be necessary to consult with school staff, club leaders, and/or friends, and will it be advisable to observe the child or young person at school? The adolescent's social network is a changing one as friendships develop and wane and there is a natural distancing from parents and other carers. If these background sources are explored the therapists have to add this knowledge to their empirical experience and then make an assessment in order to plan treatment and further diagnostic work. This would involve looking at age-appropriate skills; skills that focus on cognitive and emotional functioning, together with language and motor development, seeking to discover whether there is need for further extended observations and assessments.

It will be essential to follow a course of action that is acceptable to the parents and their child. If the parents do not agree with the proposals it is likely that the juvenile with divided loyalties will find it difficult to cooperate with the therapist, but if the parents can visualise themselves as 'team members' the path will be much smoother. When a referral stems from a school or kindergarten the therapist informs the parents of the nature of the report, and will reassure them on a point of confidentiality if they request their additional comments go no further. The parents have the right to decide how much of the picture the specialists have formed is to be given to others. Before outlining a particular case I wish to explain the basis for the diagnostic work.

The A.M.S. Method

The technique used in Norway is known as the A.M.S. Method, having been developed at the University of Oslo by Professor Emeritus Anne-Marit Sletten Duve. This educational assessment model is based upon a psychoanalytic personality-structure model. The concepts of ego (the

'I', i.e. our sense of self), id (our instincts or drive) and superego (our conscience) playing major roles in this intrapsychic model. Put briefly, the method is to observe how the child reacts in a learning situation. Is the child stressed, inhibited or does it react in an ordinary way?

The method is primarily used as a tool for clinical educational therapists to assist in diagnosing children and adolescents with psychological problems, within an educational environment. (Professor Duve thinks it is important to give the room to be used an 'educational bias' as it is in rooms that are similar that the child or young person has previously 'failed'.). This technique analyses the children's learning abilities linked to their emotional bond to learning. The method maps ego-resources and ego-strengths.

The A.M.S. method is in six stages and includes a number of categories with a set of variables:

Stage I – Educational life-space

The concept of life-space was first introduced by Kurt Lewin in 1935. Lewin was interested in studying how life-space or 'inner world' influenced a child's psychological existence. Duve's reason for using the concept of life-space in an educational situation was to help the clinician or observer to be aware of how, and in what way, a particular 'schoolroom' affects a child's personality structure.

Stage II – Educational superego

This stage focuses on a child's behaviour when together with an authority figure. The child's interactive behaviour with an adult can give the educational therapist an idea of the quality of a child's ego strength. 'Ego-strength' means to what degree a child or young person gives the impression of having a positive sense of self, an awareness of age-appropriate self-esteem – they know who they are and where they belong. Those who demonstrate some degree of ego 'failure' seem to have a less sure sense of self, low self-esteem and do not know who they are or where they belong. Sometimes their behaviour indicates what Dockar-Drysdale (1993) refers to as 'an unintegrated state'.

A child's reaction to contact with the adult mirrors an inner balance or imbalance. In a school situation the child must constantly adapt to their superego (conscience indicating some sense of right and wrong). The pupil role includes, among other functions, organising one's own ego (self), superego and id (drive to achieve an aim) to the external educational superego, (i.e., their teacher) (Duve, 1974). Duve explains this by proposing that a child's reaction to contact stimulation mirrors the inner balance and degree of basic trust.

Stage III – Educational reality

In the third stage of organisation the child is interviewed about the school situation. Questions to pre-schoolers are related to the child itself, the family and the home environment.

Stage IV – Educational achievements

The fourth stage of organisation challenges the child's ability to achieve when confronted with educational tasks. The intra-psychic structures are mobilised positively or negatively when confronted with achievement demands.

Stage V – Testing the limit

In the fifth stage of organisation the child is subjected to stress in order to obtain a clearer picture of the inner structure; both its abilities and weaknesses. To ask a child to do better on a task can tell the observer something about the quality of the child's ego- strength when subjected to pressure.

Stage VI – Anxiety reduction and ego-support

This stage shows how a child profits from anxiety-reducing comments like, 'It's all right if you can't manage', and ego-supporting remarks such as, 'You did well on that one'.

Four Categories of Children

By taking into account the A.M.S.'s variables it is possible to place the children in four categories (Figure 4.1):

A   The ego-strong and emotionally healthy pupil will be found near the ego-axis, and has an adequate control functioning.

B   The ego-weak pupil will be found in the upper part away from the ego-axis with a 'failure of control'.

C   The very neurotic pupil will be found in the lower part away from the ego-axis, with over-control and rigidity which indicate a learning block.

D   The unstable and partly ego-weak pupil will be found on both sides of the ego-axis, being inconsistent and having both lack of control and over-control.

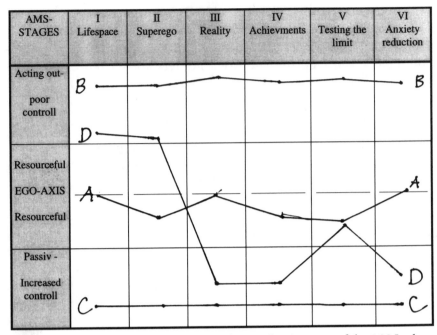

AMS-STAGES	I Lifespace	II Superego	III Reality	IV Achievments	V Testing the limit	VI Anxiety reduction

Figure 4.1 Active inner organisation according to the six stages of the A.M.S. observation method.

The A.M.S. Technique as a Clinical Educational Instrument

Additionally, the A.M.S. technique is used to develop an appropriate educational programme in school and pre-school and has been utilised in research projects and masters' theses at the University of Oslo. Since 1982, four projects have been carried through (Bjerknes Tolsa, 1982), Abrahamsen, 1983, Marstrander, 1991). The research outcomes of these projects confirm that the A.M.S. is a valid clinical educational instrument.

I have chosen my interaction with two examples to demonstrate how the A.M.S. method is used diagnostically with a pre-school and a school child.

Liv: a four-year-old girl with arthritis

This A.M.S. observation report is about Liv, a pre-school girl, 4.1 years old, suffering from *juvenile rheumatoid arthritis*. Liv contracted this illness when she was two years old.

In addition to her illness Liv was not interested in making contact with other children; she wanted to play alone. She would have preferred to stay at home sitting on the sofa with her toy animals for long periods.

Sometimes she would suddenly fly into a rage for no apparent reason. At home she wanted to override both her parents and her sisters. When the mother talked about hospitals in connection with her treatment, she would deny or refuse to take part in this conversation by walking away or turning her back on her mother. She displayed the same behaviour at the kindergarten.

Stage I – Educational life-space

Liv's mother accompanied her to the nursery. I had already met Liv and we had talked about what we would be doing. Liv went over to the sand-pit and stood beside it. She looked alternately at me and at the sand, but she just stood there until I told her to sit down. According to the A.M.S. method score she showed increased control, and was slow, anxious, shy, expectant.

Stage II – Educational superego

When Liv was told to sit down she did so immediately. When her mother left at the beginning of both observation sessions Liv asked her for her 'zebra' (a plastic toy animal). She started before I had explained what we were going to do. When I asked her to wait, she did so. When she encountered difficulties, she bent over so that her head practically touched the table, but did not ask for help. She gave no apparent sign of wanting to accept help when I offered. Here she showed resourceful-ness, interest and increased control, and was despondent, shy – timid.

Figure 4.2 Liv. Drawing of a girl in Goodenough Draw-a-Man-Test.

Stage III – Educational reality

The following questions had to be solved:

- Does this little girl realistically answer questions from the form and during conversation?
- Does she show a realistic understanding of the world in her play?

When asked if she was called anything more than Liv, she whispered, 'I don't know that much.' She knew her age but when asked the name of the place where she lives, she replied, 'I can't really say'. She could tell me that her house is white. When asked who she lived with, she answered, 'It's not easy to explain everything'.

Liv pointed correctly to five out of the six pictures in answer to the questions: What do we cook food on? What shines in the sky at night? What do we use when it rains? Where do we get milk from? What catches rats and mice? The last question was about cats and rabbits and when asked which has the longer ears she pointed to the cat and not the rabbit. Asked why we have houses she responded, with a smile, 'That's a bit difficult to say' – but she knew that books are for reading. She showed on the A.M.S. scoring resourcefulness: reality, answers to teaching reality and increased control: do not know, conceals.

Stage IV – Educational achievements

How does Liv react to tasks at the table, to free play, physical action and ball games? Liv scored above her chronological age on the Goodenough Draw-a-Man Test (Goodenough, 1926), but, her score on the Bo-Ege, Language Test 1 (Bo-Ege, 1985) corresponded to 3.0 years. The cut-out shapes were correctly arranged on the board; she succeeded with the four, age-appropriate jigsaw puzzles; copied the shapes of a circle, a square and a cross, and knew the difference between the smallest circle and the largest square.

When set the task of cutting out a circle and a square Liv struggled hard to get it right but chose to cut strips rather than the shapes. As she cut the strips she was absorbed by the action of the scissors and said several times that they were 'a great mouth that bites'. After a while she said that she did not want to continue as she was worn out. With great effort she copied the circle, square and cross, but for each one she said, 'This is hard'. Her drawing of the human figure started with the legs and followed with the arms, hands and fingers, finishing by adding the hair to the head but omitting a part of the face (Figure 4.2). For freehand drawing she chose an outline in three colours. She answered all three questions in Kim's game correctly.

In the first session of free play Liv chose to go into the doll's corner. She laid the table and served me with 'food' from the fridge, continually giving me new dishes. Whilst making the food she showed me some doctor's things which she wanted to try, and mentioned that she had just had a blood test but did not want to talk about it, interrupting me by asking if I wanted some more to eat. In the second session she decided to play with animals in the sandpit. She placed the strong animals in one group and the bad ones in another: when they fight the strong ones win – just as she had loudly and clearly predicted!

In each of these first two sessions the game had to stop because time had run out. According to the A.M.S. score she showed very good resourcefulness, but also some increased control.

Stage V – Testing the limit

Here Liv's response varied in accordance with each set task. The jigsaw puzzle was tackled immediately; if she could not fit a piece at once she was eager to keep trying. She looked up and smiled at me each time she completed a puzzle and behaved similarly during exercises where she had to point at pictures. She was slower in starting the drawing exercises, and took pauses to say she did not think that it was easy. Sometimes she asked if she could 'leave off' (stop the task), and on one occasion she asked for an eraser to rub out her drawing and added that they make fun of her 'because she makes squiggles'. In the transitions between structured and unstructured play she offered no resistance. At the beginning of the first two sessions she asked to have her 'zebra' beside her.

She set to work immediately on any new exercise but where she had to talk about herself and her family she gave few answers, commenting that she did not think that it was easy to answer these questions. At the end of this first session when I asked if she thought it had been fun, she simply nodded her head. She liked drawing best and thought that throwing the big ball was silly as she preferred a small one. She thought it had been difficult but said she would have liked to continue. On the A.M.S. score she showed mostly resourcefulness, some increased control and also some poor control.

Stage VI–Anxiety reduction and ego-support

How does Liv react to anxiety-reducing comments like, 'It doesn't matter if you can't do it', or self-boosting remarks such as, 'That was well done', or, 'You did that well'?

When Liv struggled with a task and was told it did not matter if she could not do it, she carried on unconcerned. When praised with, 'You did that well', she smiled and looked down at the table and continued at a faster pace. On the A.M.S. score she showed equal parts of resourcefulness and increased control.

Table 4.1 Summary of the A.M.S. scores: Liv.

A.M.S. stages		I	II	III	IV	V	VI
Indi-vidu-al	Poor control					1	
	Resourceful	1	2	5	3	3	3
	Increased control	4	2	2	1	1	3

Conclusions

The conclusions from my observations and the assessment of the tests suggested that Liv's emotional state was repressed in spite of large resources. Liv seemed to be too insecure to express her aggressive feelings, and I felt that the right approach in this case would be to work with the kindergarten and her home with the aim of gradually building her self-esteem. My aim would be to try to reduce her feelings of insecurity, thus increasing her self-confidence and ability to express her emotions without impairing the skills she has acquired.

In this case cooperation between the home and the kindergarten was of great importance. The parents and the staff at the kindergarten needed to get a deeper understanding of the reason for this repressed behaviour and the possibilities of reducing it. They were recommended to support Liv during her aggressive periods and try to stimulate her positive resources as shown in the A.M.S. observation.

The observations made during play in the sandpit showed this clearly. At first she was very shy, but later she played with creativity which included aggressive play with the animals. It is important for the grown-ups to try to structure this aggressive play and also to choose the right material for playing. Fingerpainting, for instance, is an unstructured play and can therefore be provocative for children of this type. To help her further with her behaviour problems, it is absolute necessary for the parents and the staff at kindergarten to have good contact with the child, that is to become more aware of her needs and wishes.

Per: a Nine-year-old Boy with Social, Emotional and Learning Disabilities

This A.M.S. observation report is about Per, a nine-year-old boy with social, emotional and learning disabilities. According to the teacher, he started to show this behaviour when he started school at the age of seven.

Per showed a high level of activity both at school and home. In addition he was uneasy and lacked concentration. When losing a game or competition he reacted with anger. He had frequent fights with his classmates. His ability to read was weak, but he was better at mathematics. He had problems with having someone to decide for him; he liked to decide everything for himself. His mother and the school wanted to have an observation by an educational therapist.

Before the observation I had a conversation with Per and his parents and observed him in the classroom. Per came for the pedagogic observation together with his mother. He waited to enter into the room until I opened the door. He said goodbye to his mother in an ordinary way, being much more concerned about what was going to happen during the observation than saying goodbye to his mother.

Stage I – Educational life-space

When Per entered the room he looked around, asking where he should place his coat. During this sequence he appeared confident, observant and interested, but at the same time he gave the impression of being confused and uneasy. The movement of his body and the fact that he talked all the time, made him look stressed as if he was short of time. A striking thing was his hoarse voice. Sometimes he even chose to whisper; then it was difficult to understand every word. There were hardly any breaks for breathing.

Figure 4.3 Per. Drawing of a boy seen from behind in Goodenough Draw-a-Man-Test.

According to A.M.S. diagnosis he showed the following resources: interested, confident, observant, but also ill at ease and hectic in manner.

Stage II – Educational superego

When Per was asked to sit down on the chair, he did that at once. He took the pencil and asked what he was going to do. During the conversation about school he was uneasy and had difficulty in sitting quietly on the chair. He fingered all the items on the table within his reach. He showed the following resources: interested, normal contact, confident, but also showed a restlessness in his motor control.

Stage III – Educational reality

He was then asked several questions about his school situation. Per had adequate answers to the questions and they were delivered without hesitation. He could describe what was difficult and what was not difficult at school. According to A.M.S. diagnosis he showed concrete and realistic behaviour.

Stage IV – Educational achievements

How does Per react to tasks at the table? He had difficulties with the orthography in writing and used the eraser frequently. He had difficulties in remembering sentences being dictated for him to write down. He often wondered how he should write the different words. His reading was erratic. When he got to words he could not pronounce, he asked for assistance. He remembered well what he had read. He had to have a great deal of help with reading; if he was not given any, he stopped totally.

Two tests were given to assess Per's maturity age. The Bender Motor Gestalt Test (Bender, 1938) showed a maturity age of 7.6 years. He often diminished the figures which could signify anxiety. In Goodenough's Draw-A-Man Test (Goodenough, 1926) he was very doubtful about what he could manage. At first he drew a boy seen from behind (Figure 4.3), then a girl from the front. According to this test his maturity age was 9 years.

In the mathematical tasks he worked faster and with greater confidence. He showed several aspects of his resources, but also showed areas where he struggled, i.e., poor concentration and difficulty in understanding the task.

Stage V – Testing the limit

When given tasks of writing and drawing, which he evidently had problems in doing, Per showed positive sides such as good contact, but on the more negative side, unease and lack of concentration.

Stage VI – Anxiety reduction and ego-support

How does Per react to anxiety-reducing comments such as: 'It doesn't matter if you cannot do it' or self-boosting remarks such as: 'That was well done' or 'You did that well!' By such remarks he became more secure and the unease diminished.

Table 4.2 Summary of the A.M.S. scores: Per.

A.M.S. stages		I	II	III	IV	V	VI
Indi-vidu-al	Poor control	2	1		2	2	
	Resourceful	3	3	5	4	2	2
	Increased control				1		

Conclusion

The conclusion from this observation showed that Per had many resources, but he also showed tendencies to poor control. It was important to reduce the anxiety related to achievements, especially his concerns with writing and drawing. It was decided to investigate whether his bad eye/hand coordination (Bender, 1938) was because of neurological reasons. The school started special writing lessons for him alone with a teacher.

In the talks with the parents I changed from general topics to more specific topics such as making an agenda for his day. Such a plan can be a safety-creating factor and help to reduce the demands of the parents on their child. It was important to reduce the demands made by school-work by encouraging non-school activities with father or mother at home.

The ability to write improved slowly. Per became, at the same time, less of a clown, and there were fewer fights with his classmates. He said that he would rather use his time for playing.

Chapter 5
Working Independently or as a Member of a Team

ANNIKEN MARSTRANDER

The Different Techniques Used with Individuals, Groups, Parents, and Kindergarten and School Teachers

There are several ways of carrying out treatment, as we call our work in Norway. That is probably why our profession seems so exciting and varied. Behaviour problems of one child or adolescent may seem to be similar to that of another, but their emotional reaction patterns may be quite different. Inner and outer restlessness varies considerably according to different situations in which children or adolescents find themselves.

My experience includes work with pre-schoolers like Liv (chapter 4). The techniques and methods I use, and will be discussing throughout this chapter, have roots in the special-therapeutic psychodynamic explanation theory of Anne-Marit Duve (1965). This is for the treatment of emotional development and satisfaction of needs that may, for example, be irrationally linked with profound anxiety and blocks to learning (Duve, 1965). It is natural to wish to clarify the state of a child's or young person's present knowledge and competence level compared with their age and abilities. A closer knowledge of their anxieties and their abilities provides hypotheses about the function of the interaction between learning problems and psychodynamics, on which a pedagogical treatment programme can be set up (Duve, 1965).

A treatment programme focuses on several areas; teamwork with parents, kindergarten or school staff. We have spent considerable time in figuring out at what point our specialised educational therapeutic approach should be introduced. The manner and the range of our participation is another question that is not always easy to answer. Many thoughts and reflections are considered before we choose the treatment strategy for a child and their environment. Our intention is to find a therapeutic approach that activates the conflict-free areas of functioning that have remained unharmed in each child. Children with adaptation problems are described as labile (unstable) and restless by Duve; such behaviour she believes reduces achievements. The appetite to learn is activated when a focus can be directed towards the unharmed function areas. Duve, a psychologist, suggests six techniques that educational therapists keep in mind when they accept children for treatment. Their aim is to reduce anxiety as a means of reducing learning resistance. She feels that if all educational therapists master these techniques their professional skills will be accepted in any psychiatric/psychological environment, and states, 'Training in psychodynamics is necessary in order to arrive at a complete understanding of the connections between the child's emotional, cognitive, and social development' (Duve, 1965). I will comment upon these techniques.

1. A strengthening of defence mechanisms – in relationship to ego-strong defence mechanisms – rather than a weakening of defence mechanisms.

When people are threatened they become, naturally enough, frightened. This fear and anxiety overwhelms us; we feel uncomfortable. The discomfort may, at times, be so psychologically painful that we find mechanisms to reduce and defend against the pain.

To build up a network of defence mechanisms in personality structures is a central task emphasised in a therapist–child interaction relationship. Often an imbalance has developed between the various types of defence mechanisms that the child is equipped with in order to defend and protect the ego or inner self. Anger, acting-out, and get-it-out feelings are emotional reactions that we have all experienced, to a lesser or greater extent, when we have been exposed to threats 'attacking' our ego-existence.

Aggression is an emotional reaction that functions as a defence mechanism to reduce anxiety. Restlessness, concentration difficulties, and attention failure are other defence mechanisms available to reduce anxiety. These are reactions that may arise when the psychological discomfort takes too much space in a child's inner life. Restlessness may appear as physical or mental thought, and it may be necessary for the child to make use of restlessness in order to be able to grow up as others have determined they should. But we know that too much of this behaviour over a period of time may prevent the child from positive development. Our task as therapists is, therefore, to channel this behaviour into appropriate forms of interaction.

We know that primitive and poor defence mechanisms have an active rub-off effect on most aspects of our personality. Children who are being treated by us must be able to understand that they can express their emotions. To accept emotional reactions that protect our ego is important. The children who are accepted for treatment are often upset and

frustrated, ashamed of their overwhelming anger towards those closest to
them, themselves and their environment. Our task is to find out what is
being expressed by their behaviour. Where does the child suffer their real
problems? What is the origin of the conflict in the child's personality structure?

One example is Ruth who stamped upon her teddy bear to show her
anger although she had been a nice, smiling and polite girl. It is important to support her during these outbursts to relieve the pressure on her.
A child needs to be unchained from emotional disturbances that hinder
or block their eagerness to learn, their ability to show curiosity and
creative zest. Psychologist Daniel Stern says that adults should give the
child the real experience of their own image which should dominate our
everyday life. 'It is the experience of one's own image that acts, it is the
ego that senses emotions, it is the ego that has intentions, that plans, it is
the ego that "translates" emotions into language, it is the ego that
communicates and passes on personal knowledge' (Stern, 1985).

Children with a dominating defence mechanism for reducing anxiety
have little or no experience of their own image. The task for the therapist is to re-establish the child's image. How can we do this in such a way
that this may, in the course of time, be felt not occasionally but every day
in a continuum? We must encourage the child to develop their inner
resources, not only when they are alone, but also when in company. The
ego-strength has, eventually, to dominate, but for most of the children
who are referred to us, their ego-weakness is a heavy burden to take
further along in life.

The educational therapist aims to help children to achieve constructive defence mechanisms and prevent the primitive defence mechanisms
from dominating. If the experience of one's own image is seriously
weakened this will disturb social functioning. 'A personality without a
structure leads to chaos, which again results in poor socialization'
(Stern, 1985). Primitive emotional states may arise when the child's
achievements are threatened. Fear of non-achievement may cause
regression or projection; it may interrupt an activity; it may lead to
denial, intellectualisation, repression, phobia or desperation. These
behaviour patterns, or defence mechanisms, tell us that our emotional
reactions vary when facing anxiety. The degree of these emotional states
compared with the degree of learning resistance may give us some information as to the correspondence between the child's learning problems
and the child's psychodynamic functioning.

2. Reducing anxious feelings rather than provoking them

How can this be done? How can anxiety that has almost become a part of
the child's inner life be reduced? Our attitude, as adults, is of major
importance: the child must, from the first moment, feel accepted; we

refrain from arranging activities that remind the child of achievement loss (this also reduces anxiety). A therapeutic room can produce bad memories, and reduce self-esteem that may be instrumental in aggravating a feeling of inferiority. The choice and type, quality and amount of material or equipment is essential with respect to promoting learning and preventing further blocking of the child's hidden learning skills, and may also increase or reduce the loss of self-esteem.

Children of pre-school and early-school age begin with a workbook with their name on it, and a tube of glue. Postcards are often used, with pictures of, for example, farm and wild animals. It is an activity which does not depend on a great deal of fantasy, but gives interesting results.

Choosing materials for adolescents can be more challenging. The art and craft materials may embarrass adolescents because it takes some time to 'warm them up'. I find that a conversation around their own interest areas (hobbies, motorcycles, friends, sports, clothes and so on) provides a focus and shows that I am interested in them as individuals and can empathise with their difficulties.

3. Making use of children's imaginative play

One must not make interpretations, but rather take advantage of the imaginative material presented is Duve's third technique for achieving good educational therapeutic treatment. What does she mean by this?

Several psychoanalysts have pointed out that interpreting directly to the child easily leads to misinterpretations. For the child this may be felt as confusing rather than informative. We make interpretations to ourselves, or with team members, but not directly to the client. When we have made a discovery, or when we think we have found it, we may try a careful presentation of this interpretation to the client. But this must be done very carefully; we could be wrong, which might cause an aggravation or escalation of existing psychological disorders. Time with a pre-schooler or primary school child should rather be spent using 'imaginative material'. The child's play represents imagination and can lead to a better understanding of the child's reality. The child may show in their play that the baby toy animals are afraid and need to be looked after by the mother animal. The educational therapist may ask if the babies are afraid and need to be with their mother. What the child here presents may be their reality. To myself I might interpret that this message represents, 'Is the child asking for more attention from Mother?' or: 'Is the child expressing how important it is to have a mother who can, or cannot, give comfort?'

4. Preventing destructive activity

In her fourth technique, Duve stresses the importance of distracting, preventing, stopping, and discouraging destructive play. Children or adolescents who come for treatment are often destructive in their behaviour, either towards themselves or towards their environment. We know that a behaviour pattern like this is destructive in itself. It tears down one's feeling of dignity. After such an act we know for certain that the self-esteem is injured. In other words, if we are to strengthen the self-respect, actions like these must be avoided. Some suggestions towards avoiding them include removing broken toys, limiting the number of toys, and offering an opportunity for discovering what may be of interest to them. Better order – that is not too many stimuli – may be of help to reduce inner restlessness. In my experience, fewer stimuli may also be instrumental in strengthening some children's constructive creativity, and the child may become more self-assertive.

For example, when the teacher asks Roy to find his book in his bag, he notices it is damaged and that the pencil and eraser are missing. It is important to explain to the teacher, parents, and Roy how important it is for Roy to have his schoolbooks in order. If not he will show increased unrest and be more destructive.

5. How to reduce feelings of conflict and destructive behaviour

The fifth technique, Duve stresses, is one which must not touch upon any reasons for conflict and destruction, but reduce the effect as far as possible. My brief comment to this is that we know that spending time with clients, regarding the causes (the what? and why?) can have negative results when our aim is to build up positive relationships. By spending time on this topic I think we are in danger of reintroducing to the child a previously experienced psychological discomfort. Distraction, on the contrary, may help the child turn away from the discomfort.

Another technique is to reduce the revealed or expressed emotional message which could then prevent a flourishing of previously felt unpleasant events. For example, Ruth, a victim of bullying in her kindergarten, cries every morning. She is afraid of Kari who pushes her. When this is explained to the staff in the kindergarten with suggestions on how they should face this problem, things change. Ruth gradually feels safe enough to show her feelings and needs. Months later in the treatment, Ruth masters her fears and manages a more genuine contact with the other children.

6. When to point out specific incidents to reduce negative attitudes

The sixth, and last, technique is: one should only use pointing-out in quite specific situations as a means of reducing the effect of negative attitudes on the child's constructive development. Pointing out should only be used when the child exhibits negative behaviour that could inhibit the development of a more positive and constructive way of behaving and learning. We are again reminded that a constructive development must be protected and shielded. In other words, a negative behaviour must be stopped in order to give the child's resources scope to develop.

An educational therapist (Bjerknes Tolsa, 1982), who is also a secondary school teacher, gives examples in her MA thesis of how a teacher should react when facing different types of defence mechanisms for reducing anxiety. Ivan, eight years old, is running and shouting into the classroom early in the morning. The teacher goes to him but does not speak. She is facing a pupil with restlessness (poor control over behaviour). Ivan may be helped if we suggest to the teacher that he is given a lot of attention once the lesson starts, because restlessness generally is a disturbing element. Being aware that this behaviour not only causes interruptions but that it provokes anxiety may result in developing different adult attitudes and understanding. Knowing what this restlessness expresses is not of major importance in the initial stages of the treatment, but it proved that this kind of help had a further positive effect on teaching later, on that and subsequent days at school.

Secondly, Sol, a 10-year-old girl, is sitting close to the window far back in the classroom, 'nice', smiling and quiet. The teacher moves her to another desk close to herself, and starts talking to her. By the end of the lesson Sol gives answers. This concerns a pupil with inhibited behaviour, i.e., she over-controls her impulses. Behaviour like this often leads to learning resistance. Tolsa stresses that these pupils need extra attention, care, and support from the teacher. Encouragement from, and contact with, the teacher are good tools (Bjerknes Tolsa, 1982). The therapist must help teachers to increase the child's ego-strength and not tear down the defence mechanisms.

Methods of Treatment

The question of which methods we use in our treatment is difficult to answer. By method we are also talking about which tools we choose. It is quite obvious that after several years of experience working with pre-schoolers in particular there are certain tools that I use more often than others. The reason why a particular method is chosen in connection with each child may seem random, but it is not necessarily so.

In the pedagogical psychological dictionary the term 'method' is defined as 'a systematic course of action'. 'Educational therapists contribute towards a child becoming a person who feels comfortable with themselves and with others, who is able to develop in play and work, who has a realistic picture of reality, and who is able to make use of their social and intellectual skills' (Holdhus, 1987). The theoretical frame of reference is based on an understanding of how a pedagogical environment affects the child's inner psychological processes. The systematic course of action or method applied by most educational therapists is interwoven with psychodynamic theories. Thus, the theory is not only to understand the individual child's needs, but is actively introduced by use of object relations theory, which again has its roots in psychoanalytic theory of instincts. Freud has written about the relationship between the ego and the object (Freud, 1931) and considers the mother figure as the primary object. A relationship between a child's ego, that is the sense of self, and the object, that is the adult, is attained when the adult demonstrates a capability of catching the child's signals (Abrahamsen, 1983).

The educational therapist's approach is similar to the insight of a child psychiatrist and their intervention can strengthen and expand the resource areas within the child, i. e., the ego-strengths the child already possesses. The therapist is therefore a person who can reduce, and possibly prevent, an aggravation of psychogenic resistance to learning. The method or technique we use is where ego-strengthening therapy is in focus; when an ego-weak child in the course of time becomes an ego-strong child. But primary needs must be satisfied before we will see positive changes in the child's ability to open up and become receptive to learning. Can the zest to learn become as natural as the zest for something good to eat? A child's eagerness provides stimuli for further cognitive development.

The initial stages of the educational therapeutic work are most important and central with respect to contact establishment between the adult and the child. A positive reciprocal influence between the child's built-in maturity pattern and the surrounding environment is of major importance for further learning. This reciprocal influence may only be achieved when the therapist knows the child's ego-strength or ego-weakness. 'The child's ego-strength or ego-weakness should be assessed in view of a development aspect in a social and emotional connection' (Abrahamsen, 1983).

Positive reciprocal influence once established, is conducive to diagnostic work concerning the areas that the therapist, in cooperation with the child, emphasises in the treatment. A dynamic interaction is a positive interaction and will be instrumental in transferring knowledge beyond the areas where this knowledge is, at this point, being revealed. Once established, the child may more easily accept being guided, and be more cooperative and less resistant to gaining new skills.

'Emotional new learning' is a phrase that Valborg Holdhus (1987) introduces when she describes characteristics of an educational therapeutic treatment. It means the changing of an emotional image of oneself. It is of major value that the child's self-esteem is built up, which gives a positive self-image, whether the feeling is one of happiness, of being at ease with self, or even of sadness.

I have outlined theoretical techniques to be used within educational therapeutic treatment. How, then, can they be carried out in reality when one is not supposed to touch upon causes of conflicts and destruction, but reduce their effect as far as possible? It is one thing to know these techniques, but another thing to know how to apply them when facing the child in question. The method here is to work on the child's inner conflictual world in an indirect rather than in a direct way. As mentioned above, we know that a direct approach towards difficult emotional experiences will aggravate primitive and negative defence mechanisms rather than encourage constructive defence mechanisms (Duve, 1965).

In work with pre-schoolers, play has been used as an indirect way of working on a child's inner conflict. Play may be instrumental in abreacting the power of the experience and conquering anxiety and conflicts. It, in itself, is an effective way of working on anxiety-ridden experiences, and is also important for the development of the child's need to adapt to their environment. Puppets and a theatre present an invaluable opportunity for the child to venture into encroaching areas of conflict. Some of these feelings can be placed into a puppet which can express them within the play – thus making them less threatening to the child. It is the third person (the puppet) who expresses the problem. This distance may permit the child to participate, and reflect more actively concerning their own emotional reactions. The theme of the play may, for example, be that of not being included among a group of friends.

It is important that the metaphor (the play) has a special meaning compared to the child's situation – it must be personally relevant. This may happen when the metaphor confirms something about the child's perception of their own situation (Mossige, 1993).

Another type of metaphor is used in drawing. Making a drawing with the child may reveal problem areas thought to be relevant to the child. A drawing of, for example, a happy or an angry emotion, or an 'I-am-sad' emotion may alert the child's attention to their own psychological state. The drawing may thus have a reparative, healing effect in itself if a child can become more familiar with feelings and venture into those aspects of themselves that have been, or still are, psychologically painful.

A method like this for further work on psychological disorders may be instrumental in freeing up static emotional disorders. 'The metaphor must convey the idea that a form of change or movement is possible and that the subject has the resources necessary for setting this development off' (Mossige, 1993).

Children or Young People in a Group Setting

We know that often because of previous negative experiences with functioning in a group, children or adolescents show great resistance to the setting up of a group process. The educational therapist's belief that a group can change and focus on a secure, confident atmosphere in the group, are factors that are imperative for the implementation of a dynamic group process.

Interdependence is a keyword that should all the time be granted respect. The size of the group, the number of hours per session, and how often it should get together, are factors that must be planned in advance. The age, the sex, and the types of behaviour patterns are other factors that must be considered.

Most of the children referred to a group are functioning immaturely in a social setting. They have difficulties in relating constructively to their peers and adults. Being able positively to give something to others and positively to get or receive something from others is difficult. In these groups social contacts are usually rejected, thus preventing social interactions that are imperative for further positive relations between members.

I have experience of working with children between the ages of three to six years, for four hourly sessions on a daily basis. (The duration of the group treatment is one to two years.) The rest of their day is spent in the kindergarten. The time given offers them resources to manage the other situations in their daily life. The behaviour disorders have been of a varied nature. Children with acting-out behaviour have been represented most frequently during my 11 years as a group therapist. Children with inhibited behaviour, with psychosomatic diseases, with linguistic difficulties, and understimulated children are some of the other behaviour patterns represented. Placing too many children with similar behaviour in the same group produces poorer results than if the group has had a more balanced composition. A clear majority of one particular type of behaviour may thus have the effect of stigmatising the children's problem area rather than having the intended redeeming effect. Each child in time will gradually reveal their resources to the other members of the group. If they meet many children with a similar behaviour pattern, this may be felt as threatening. Several restless children together can have a destructive rather than a positive effect upon one another. A group that functions well may, for instance, consist of one child who is afraid of being bullied, another who bullies, a third who is afraid of playing and some who come from less resourceful families.

What the child may more easily be able to see and understand are behaviour patterns that differ from the pattern that they are struggling with themselves. We know that children are very tolerant and that they, on the whole, respect others when they are provided with an explanation as to the reason for this behaviour. What is critical here is the group leader's behaviour, i.e., the adult's reaction and interaction to the problems presented in the group when aiming to ease interactions.

The composition of the group is determined by the group leader. The number of children in the group should not be too high or too low; three may be too small. The reason for this is that when three children are playing together they do not always play well together at the same game and one is often excluded. Even though the group leader may be an active participant, this does not cover the child's real need, which is to play with peers.

Personally, I prefer a group of five children. This size, which is also used by many others, has allowed for greater variation without being too large. It offers the opportunity for children to establish some independence and to display initiative in relating to other children. Too many adults (two are ideal), or too few children may deprive the children of their chance to participate in the forming of a group. Age also plays a major role because the children may make use of each other's knowledge and level of mastery. But too great a spread of age in the group may block a positive group process.

How often and for how long a group treatment like this should continue depends on the degree of the behaviour disorders and, not least, on the motivation for being able to receive such treatment. I think considerable time is required for those children who, for several years, have struggled with major behaviour disorders and who have proved to have difficulties in adapting themselves to any mainstream institution, whether this is a kindergarten or a school.

In Norway we also work with small groups once a week for about two hours per session. Again, the duration depends on the extent of the problem. It is important that we are critical in our evaluation of the child's ability for self-healing.

What most children with psychological disorders have in common is, as we know, their social difficulties. Daily work on their problems in a small group over a long period of time may be instrumental in reducing negative behaviour patterns and changing them on a long-term basis. A positive change can create permanent qualitative changes in the child's personality structure. Group treatment of pre-schoolers in our clinics has demonstrated the possibilities of these altered positive structures that help children to reach more constructive interactions. Eventually children will not only feel more comfortable within themselves but also be able to give to others, and, furthermore, can then feel more comfortable when receiving something good themselves. We find group treatment has often resulted in diminishing or ending destructive attitudes.

To become less self-condemning is a desired aim in this treatment; to help children become less deprecatory, or able to tolerate rejection when facing persons who mean a lot to them, is another important aspect of this kind of treatment. Group treatment too can be instrumental in helping a child to get out of excessive loneliness. Venturing to stand up, to take one's own interests and values more seriously, are issues that are often worked on during the group process. As an example we can mention Ole who daily sat at the table with his jigsaw puzzle while the others were playing, until he was encouraged to give signals that showed he wanted to take part in their play.

For the numerous aspects of the personality that are subject to atten-tion in a group we try to make links during all the interactions. The aim is to increase insight into one's own role in group situations: it enhances the individual's experience of personal participation in psychosocial interaction. In this climate the educational therapist functions as a cata-lyst and should therefore be able to pick up the signals from the social game that is taking place in the group. It is challenging and exciting to work with groups!

Teamwork with Parents

What should be emphasised in respect to teamwork with parents when the child has been referred to a psychiatric clinic for children and adoles-cents? What, how much, and in what way should feedback be given? How may parents and the educational therapist find an accord that stim-ulates mutual teamwork?

We know that the educational therapist and parents need to work interdependently in order to change the child's behaviour. Knowledge of how to make human relationships function successfully is of great value. With professional competence the therapist is in a position to arrange the situation so that parents feel able to cooperate with the insti-tution in question. We need to find a common platform where both parties can venture to stand and, in the course of time, discover that the situation is not threatening. If there is no motivation for continuing to try to change from negative to positive behaviour, there needs to be a mutually agreed point of no return.

Most parents who have given their consent to a referral to a psychi-atric clinic for children and adolescents are, to begin with, motivated for teamwork. It is important that the aims of the therapist and the parents are clear and agree, if we are to establish a dialogue and not a mono-logue. We try to arrange a climate where the parents are encouraged to exchange opinions, and, if possible, release their feelings about being someone who has not managed the task of parenting in a way that satis-fies them. Our task as members of a team is to reduce ego-weak aspects and encourage ego-strong aspects in the child and the parents. It is the children who are regarded as 'good' by the family who represent most ego-strong aspects. If the child cannot venture to make use of mastery skills it is their ego-weak aspects that are represented within the family.

There are many parents who consider themselves 'not good' and these feelings promote a feeling of inferiority. We know that the domi-nance of these feelings leaves little room for the development of a person's 'good' qualities. Therefore, it is our task to encourage the ego-strength qualities in the parents as well as in their children. Confidence and security are achieved through positive interactions where parents are given an opportunity to discover their positive resources. Uncovering these depends on the therapist's ability for empathy and insight; sensitivity is fundamental in establishing cooperation between the parents and themselves. For instance, if a son turns from his father, we must help the father to feel secure enough to accept new ways of communicating with his child.

The positive or negative effect of the teamwork can be seen in the manner in which it is received by the parents. Has the therapist created a good atmosphere, so that the parents feel motivated to work with the problem? There are several ways of expressing satisfaction. Secure parents keep appointments, take an interest in conversations and in the educational therapist's activities towards the child individually, in kindergarten, or at school. If parents express themselves positively about the educational therapist's dedication with respect to their shared plans, we can work well together. Finding that parents are open, ask questions, are problem-oriented, can venture to air their disappointment and frustrations, I also consider examples of a genuine contact between parents and the therapist.

There are other aspects to consider when we are working in a team with parents. In order to achieve the most effective teamwork, the therapist should constantly keep in mind the unpleasant situation that the parents find themselves in, and, not least, the fact that they have been in that unpleasant situation for several years. We must let them experience gradually their own positive worth before we can start demanding more stimulation of their child's linguistic and cognitive functions, or suggesting a change of routine such as bedtime, eating habits and so on.

If we succeed in encouraging the 'good enough' parents, an emphasis on a stimulation of the general personality development of the child may then become a more natural part of their upbringing. Winnicott emphasises the importance of parents who build a home and stick together, thus providing the basic ration of child care and maintaining a setting in which a child can grow up (Winnicott, 1986). The therapeutic work concerning the parents is mainly to serve to support the child's psychological structures and form a basis for the development and the changes that are under way. 'It is essential that the parents understand the child's various reactions and make arrangements so that the new behaviour potential can be channelled in a positive direction in the home environment' (Fossen and Diseth, 1991).

Teamwork with Kindergarten and School

The method used to achieve positive teamwork is theoretically based in Gerald Caplan's model which stresses how mental hygienic consultation may be carried out between mental hygiene specialists (e.g. educational therapists) and other professions, e.g. pre-school and primary school teachers. This author emphasises, in his consultation method model, the importance of good teamwork between two specialists working with a client. *Confidence*, *contact* and *contract* are factors Caplan stresses in a teamwork relationship. With his model he underlines, among other things, the need to increase the consultee's work ability and feeling of intrinsic worth which will increase after a successful consultation. 'With respect to contract, it is important to limit the duration of the consultation. The amount of time set aside is determined on the basis of the consultee's need for running help in his work problem' (Caplan, 1970).

Just as important as teamwork with parents is teamwork with kindergartens and schools. I know that there are some specialists who do not give much priority to this kind of teamwork, but I feel dependent on this kind of cooperation if I am to provide a complete treatment. The reason for the necessity of this contact with kindergartens and schools is that this is where the children spend most of their day. In a pedagogical institution the child is exposed to stimuli that may provoke, or further increase, the ego-weak aspects of their behaviour. That is why working in a team with the adults who see the child/adolescent every day is of great importance. Educational staff members may find the situation difficult; not least to understand the behaviour of, for example, a boy like Peter, aged 12 years, who throws paper balls and hard things across the classroom and cannot become a member of his peer group.

We do not always understand what is behind every single act of behaviour. Contact with an educational therapist with child psychiatric competence can lead to a better understanding of different behaviours. As a team member the teacher may more readily change previous attitudes towards the behaviour of a boy like Peter. With respect to reducing negative behaviour, we know at least that if 'poor' relations between teacher and child or adolescent and peers continues, this may lead to major problems at school, and in turn to negative behaviour in the home environment. This rub-off effect of negative behaviour could be modified, an important reason for giving priority to this kind of teamwork.

An important aspect of our active participation in the everyday life of children or young people in kindergarten or classroom, is conversations with teachers, who then feel that they are not alone with the pupil's problem behaviour: the responsibility becomes a shared one. Our professional expertise as educational therapists may be instrumental in accelerating a change of attitude in the teacher who often feels isolated with the responsibility and the problem. The teacher must be allowed to demand the extra knowledge of the educational therapists concerning the child's psychological wellbeing. We know that changes in the child's school or kindergarten environment may contribute to positive changes in the child's general behaviour.

Acknowledgement

I would like to thank educational therapist Edda Bjerknes Tolsa, Oslo, for her invaluable comments, Muriel and Harry Barrett for their help with my English, and, finally, my husband Lyder for all his support.

Part Two

Using Educational Therapy Techniques and Theoretical Concepts in the Classroom

Chapter 6
Every Picture Tells
A Story

JUDITH WATERFIELD AND ANI BROWN

Art and Educational Therapy as a Joint Approach to Group Work in an Adolescent Mental Health Unit

Preface

We worked as co-therapists with a weekly art therapy group, for four years, in a department of child and adolescent mental health; and as part of a team on an intensive day programme for adolescents with emotional and mental health problems. The unit encompasses a strong culture of multidisciplinary practice in its in-patient day treatment, and out-patient work. It incorporates psychodynamic and systemic thinking providing a broad and deep perspective on the complexities of emotions and their impact on personal development, learning and relationships.

Introduction

Our decision to run a group came from a shared perception that our professional backgrounds of teacher therapist and art therapist respectively, with common theoretical beliefs and approaches, could be integrated to meet the conflicting demands of the adolescent process, and facilitate the individuals' social, cognitive and emotional growth at a conscious and unconscious level.

We ran it as a slow, open group, i.e., ongoing sessions with new members arriving in a planned way. It comprised six young people between the ages of 15 and 19 years who were making the transition from school or training, or, from the intensive day treatment programme, to the out-patient service, and from family home to independent living.

Brief Background Stories

Dean: aged 19+

Dean joined the group as part of his continuing treatment following two years on the five-day group programme. He lived alone in a sheltered bedsitter and after a two-year training programme, and a long placement as a gardener/caretaker for a community church, he became unemployed. Some contact with his immediate family was maintained – mother, stepfather and half-sister aged 10 years, plus strong links with his maternal grandmother. Dean's natural father was unknown to him and denigrated by his mother. He had a history of high anxiety, obsessional 'odd' behaviour, and poor peer relationships. He was in a special school for slow learners until the fourth year but transferred to the local comprehensive school where his schooling broke down in the fifth year.

Tracey: aged 15+

Tracey was referred by an out-patient social worker because of repeated self-harm. The bruises and lacerations, mostly on her face, were not recognised by her mother or Tracey as having any significance. Spasmodic school attendance led to concerns about Tracey's safety. She was brought up by her maternal grandfather with regular, but brief, visits from her mother. Her grandfather remarried when she was fourteen, whereupon Tracey returned to live with her mother and her mother's partner. Neither Tracey nor her mother had had contact with her natural father since her birth. Tracey became pregnant at 16 and left the group temporarily for childbirth. Her experiences echoed those of her mother, with no acknowledgement by the baby's father during or after the pregnancy.

Louise: aged 16+

Louise was referred to the group by Ani following individual art therapy, to encourage the development of her peer relationships. The eldest child of a long-term deprived, single-parent family, she lived with her mother and sister, aged 13. Her brother aged 15 was in foster care. She was treated for ovarian cancer at 12 years old and was a rape victim at 14. Louise managed school reasonably successfully and had been entered for some GCSEs. Mother encouraged her but Louise felt this was in order to receive welfare benefits, therefore she became determined to leave and undertake Community Care Training.

Peter: aged 17

Peter attended the clinic with his family for over a year and was referred to the group by Ani following individual art therapy. He lived at home with his parents and older brother, aged 22. The eldest brother was in residential care with profound learning disabilities. The family culture was one of learning difficulties and deprivation. Peter's older sister had a history of sexual abuse by the father, who recently returned to the family following a prison sentence. Peter attended a school for special needs which was a containing and valued experience, although he still needed help with peer relationships, demonstrated poor hygiene, and was unable to control his bowel movements.

Simon: aged 15+

Simon was referred by a consultant psychiatrist after family sessions to explore his refusal to attend school during his GCSE year. Simon presented a frozen picture with no eye contact, but an occasional fleeting nervous smile. He spoke at home, was selectively mute elsewhere, and isolated from his peers at school. He lived with his parents and older and younger sisters, who were presented as having no problems. Father saw no significant cause for concern regarding Simon's withdrawal, likening this to his own adolescent behaviour.

Tom: aged 17+

Tom had a hearing and learning impairment following his mother's rubella infection during pregnancy. He was at a residential school for physically disabled children, and was referred by an out-patient therapist following an incident of inappropriate sexual activity with a much younger pupil. Tom was adopted as a baby but his special needs were not conveyed to the adoptive parents who struggled to find support for their early concerns. He had a younger, academically and socially bright, sister – the natural child of his adoptive parents. His adoptive mother had had a nervous breakdown, prior to his joining the residential school, attributed to the stress of coping and accepting Tom's behaviour.

The Purpose and Process of the Group

We aimed to provide these vulnerable adolescents with a physically and emotionally containing environment with clear boundaries of consistent space and time. The group milieu and the professional focus of each therapist allowed for internal feelings and external difficulties to be explored, 'within the working space', a concept based on Barrett's development of Winnicott's (1965) shared playing space between therapist and child. Barrett and Trevitt suggest that children recognise this space: 'conceptually, by learning that their thoughts will not be intruded upon, that the therapist will not become a smothering "or any other kind of mother" and that their need for space in which to think, talk, act, or switch off, will be respected' (Barrett and Trevitt, 1991).

We provided these adolescents with a 'working space' where they were encouraged to express themselves through a variety of art materials and stories, that would put them in touch with feelings engendered by their intense life experiences. We aimed to process and integrate these experiences and to recognise their impact on the current group process. As Case points out: 'whatever the named focus, i.e., art, play, drama or verbal therapy, all activity becomes representative communication of the relationships between child and therapist and between child and the group. All actions and activities may be invested symbolically with the personal material and through projections and identification, with the relationships in the room' (Case, 1994).

The use of symbols, metaphor, and activity allowed their current interactions and feelings to be explored indirectly and safely through the learning process. Linnesch explains: 'rather than expecting these youngsters to begin to use the art modality to investigate intrapsychic issues, the here and now of the group itself [is] the predominant process' (Linnesch, 1988).

Linnesch incorporates the thinking of Yallom who emphasises the importance of the group members remaining with the interaction. 'This focus greatly facilitates the development and the stark emergence of each member's social microcosm: it facilitates feedback catharsis, meaningful self-disclosure, and acquisition of socialising techniques' (Yallom, 1975 in Linnesch, 1988).

We believed our task was to keep this focus within the group in the face of adolescent defences against anxiety, and any destructive impulses revealed in their aggression, control or verbal attacks. The artistic and learning metaphors enabled them to manage explorations by the control they exercised over the materials. Additionally, group members expressed their emotional needs through requests for support for course work, decision making, literacy activities, and school participation.

As co-therapists, we developed our own working space, and took a non-directive approach to enable youngsters to communicate their unconscious feelings without the inhibiting control of set tasks. Within our working group relationships we aimed to act as containers of unconscious feelings which we believed related to their experiences in infancy.

This notion of containment is not related to the more familiar meaning of controlling behaviour, but to the ability of the therapists to act as receptacles for the adolescents' feelings, receiving, accepting and bearing what is unbearable for them to experience alone. It is derived from the work of Bion (1962) who recognised that the ability to bear anxiety, to know and think about mental pain, forms the emotional basis of thinking, and offers an opportunity for change.

By our unconditional acceptance of the material that arose that the group brought from their lives outside, we communicated that we could be trusted to bear their anxiety and pain and would endeavour to understand their feelings. Feelings were reflected back to them but reintrojected in a tolerable form. By linking with others each adolescent tentatively developed their capacity to think about feelings, and explore underlying reasons for them. This approach facilitated a process of self-exploration, creativity, group interaction and communication, a growing sense of self-identity and affirmation, crucial to moves towards adulthood.

All the young people brought entrenched patterns of faulty interactions, unprocessed feelings and 'stuckness', exacerbated by their failure to manage, and a fear of growing up. As a co-therapist couple we functioned metaphorically as 'parental figures' with whom group members (siblings) could explore a different 'family/learning' experience. We believed that our symbolic 'parental' containment offered the adolescents the opportunity of a new experience i.e., 'second-chance learning', a term used by Barrett and Trevitt (1991). They liken a child's relationship with a therapist to the 'reciprocal attachment behaviour in a mother/infant dyad – first learning'. Like these authors, we too would: 'accept negative and ambivalent feelings and manage behaviour related to these feelings, keeping [them] safe, and giving a message of belief in their potential for growth' (Barrett and Trevitt, 1991).

Respective of each young person's need to be the sole focus of a parental couple, regressions to early childhood behaviour, subsequent management of intense rivalries, jealousies or envies, often left us feeling exhausted, inadequate and empty. When these feelings could be contained we glimpsed a more appropriate peer interaction. (Even while writing this chapter, it was difficult to stay with the group process and not to focus on each adolescent and their needs.)

The External Expression Of Feelings In Symbol and Metaphor and Their Impact on Psychological Development

To understand the dynamics and creative material of our group we used the following theoretical concepts from the family developmental process of Bion (1962a), Klein (1946) and Foulkes and Anthony (1984). These theorists express their beliefs through different frames of reference, but share a communality in their understanding of primary relationships, and the importance of a growing capacity in the individual to integrate early life experiences. Basic stages of emotional development link to the relationships with the mother, father, therapist couple and subsequently the outside world.

The group expressed their experience of earlier relationships by being therapist-centred in their communications, as described by Foulkes and Anthony, which correlates with Bion's assumption states of dependency, flight and fight and pairing, and Klein's paranoid/schizoid position, where the projected feelings towards the therapist couple, and other members of the group, are idealised and split between extremes of love and hate.

We believed that the adolescents recognised our acceptance of their developmental need for dependency. By use of symbolic imagery, exploratory expression, and verbal metaphor, the members would feel safe enough to give up their defensive reactions to anxiety. A move towards a more active interest and involvement with other members would lead to a more integrated, realistic perception of us as the co-therapist couple, thus allowing the process towards separation, independence, and adolescent maturity to begin.

We suggest this move appertains to the idea by Foulkes and Anthony (1984) of 'group centred functioning' where the individual therapeutic progress occurs within the context of the group milieu, with the necessary active participation of that group. This compares with Klein's more unified depressive position where responsibility is taken for feeling which has previously been split off. Bion proposes that, in this stage of functioning, the therapy group has the capacity to stay on task by exploring feelings and thinking about each other in the group. Aspects of this healthy phase, he suggests, have a common purpose and recognition of group boundaries, the members position and function in relation to the outside world, the capacity to absorb and lose new members without the 'death of the group', freedom from exclusive subgroups, and the valuing of each individual's contribution to the group.

For the first year the young people continued to function in a predominately therapist-orientated dependency state. Individuals' preoccupation seemed to be with themselves and their relationship with one or other of the therapists, resulting in voracious demands for our attention and involvement in their exploratory efforts, to the exclusion of other members. There was often an uninhibited 'talking aloud' about the process of their creation, although no verbal response was needed, just our active receptive presence. This, however, evoked an intolerance of other individuals' greedy demands for 'parental' therapist attention; or jealous rivalries would ensue, commanding notice and interpretation from us and from the group.

The material produced in this phase of development showed a common theme of singular objects, or parts of objects, dominating the imagery.

Figure 6.1 Louise's 'Sue, the Pink Pig'.

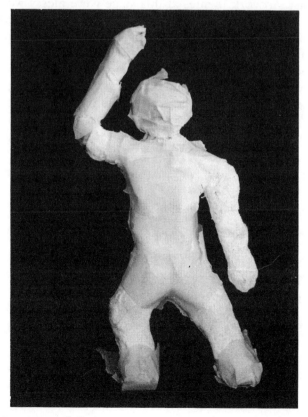

Figure 6.2 Dean's 'Footballer'.

Figure 6.3 Peter's 'Ship'.

Through the creative process the feelings communicated were alone-ness and separateness, and the desire to be 'the only one' in relation to each therapist. Artwork themes at this stage were messy work, greedy use of materials, a representation of the infant's peek-a-boo game in the creation and destruction of an image or model, the search for self, and the exploration of separation through stories, pictures and models of journeys, and modes of transport.

This stage of therapist orientation was revisited and reworked after absences, group breaks, and critical events in the adolescents' lives outside the group, e.g., illness, pregnancy, loss of job, leaving school, and change of course.

Figure 6.4 Simon's 'Puffin'.

Figure 6.5 Tracey's 'Clown'.

Figure 6.6 Tom's 'Home Alone'.

Peter

The theme of reworking and changing work in progress, which mirrored a state of internal struggle, was reflected in the work of Peter. His pattern was to create, finish, dismantle and reassemble a piece of work, but ultimately it ended in pieces (Figure 6.7). Symbolically this seemed to represent his experience of trying to repair a damaged sense of self, to achieve a different adulthood from the family pattern. This emerging self did not appear to fit the preconceived expectations of his family, but, at this stage, he was unable to understand the difference, or accept help towards a 'new' image of self. We felt that his exploration of change was related to his defence mechanism that avoided learning about the finished state of anything or coping with endings. His work seemed to express his experience of an intact family being taken apart, lost and then recreated, plus the impossibility of relationships remaining the same since the abuse of his sister. Loving and aggressive feelings shown in his artwork seemed to express ambivalent feelings towards his sister and parents. We felt this may have been stimulated by his relationships with us and the adolescent group members.

Figure 6.7 Peter's 'Van'.

Dean

Another internal struggle was exemplified by Dean's drawing of a dolls' house, which he reverted to over a period of six months, repeatedly covering it with darkening ivy leaves. Some windows and the front door were obliterated by his pen as he faced the transition of leaving his work placement with no concept of any future plans (see Figure 6.8).

Simon, Tom and Louise

Dynamic processes, alive within the group, were represented by boundary testing, a search for safety and security, and an intolerance of differences between individuals. Greenhalgh (1994) describes this intolerance of

Figure 6.8 Dean's 'Dolls' house'.

difference as a collusive defence to mask group rivalry in order to maintain a sense of safety. These were illustrated by Simon, who always started 10 minutes late, and Tom, who found it impossible to finish working by the end of sessions. We recognised this as testing what was acceptable within our 'group family'. Tom monitored the group's presences and absences in a pre-written diary and a work diary for himself in the absence of set tasks by us. He listed the towns between our unit and his home and mapped his journeys. Louise recorded a timetable for her new course. These actions and responses often echoed the fears, hopes, and explorations of others.

Each member established their own seat in the art room around the table. After a return to the group following childbirth, Tracey searched around for a re-establishment of her relationship with us by taking an empty seat, close to us, vacated by an absent member. Dean always sat in the same seat next to the same therapist. Louise tried to use all the display areas in the room for her work and pictures, as if wanting every-where to be filled by her presence and to possess us. Peter used as many materials as he could; he and Dean used the locked cupboard to store their work in between group sessions.

Scapegoating became a major theme in the early stage of the group's life. Tom was often scapegoated for his hearing difficulty, speech differences and infantile, needy attachment behaviour. We recognised this as a manifestation of the young people's fear of damage and loss of their own 'maternal' space. This developmental stage involves three defensive mechanisms – splitting, i.e., good/bad, projection, and omnipotence – to cope with powerful feelings of frustration and fear, described by Klein (1946) as 'a paranoid/schizoid position'.

We responded verbally and empathically to reflect back what was happening to the young people. Their feelings and actions were contained by us until they could know and own them for themselves, thereby internalising the experience and developing a greater capacity for individuality and thought. Other dynamic processes evident between the young people were ones of conflict, competitiveness, sharing, curiosity, domination, protectiveness and experimentation. Peter was, at times, rejecting of help from both therapists, but the results of this premature flight into independence would end in the destruction of his work. At this stage he wanted to remove all his models from the art room (possession and control), but they inevitably became damaged in transit. Louise refused to use art room material or books and brought in her own. She dominated, and was in conflict with Dean. He refused to share anything openly and put his efforts away without discussion. Tom switched off his hearing aid in order to control what he heard and avoid the need for response. Simon's flight from, and control of, relationships was manifested in his elective mutism, and his refusal of refreshments, despite his curiosity about other's work and conversations.

After a year of infantile functioning around the issues of dependency we experienced a change to 'group centred' development in their relationships, but again with regressed states being evident when choices had to be made or after change and breaks. They identified, in this phase, by creativity and verbal communications, aspects of themselves and their life experiences which they could recognise as also being owned by other group members. Fluid pairing and sharing was much in evidence with less dependency on us. The verbal attacks towards us became more playful and affectionate. Their work in this group-centred stage indicated increased flexibility, some experimentation and group imagery.

There were spontaneous expressions of thoughts, feelings and opinions with a growing but fragile sense of trust and closeness between group members and towards us. A developing appreciation, commit-

Figure 6.9 Louise's 'Family in the Park'.

Figure 6.10 Tracey's 'Circus group'.

ment, and valuing of the group appeared with an increase in personal responsibility, plus an acknowledgement of their impact on each other. Foulkes and Anthony (1984) assert that the establishment of reciprocal relationships is a clear indicator of healthy psychological development. As we have acknowledged, Klein addresses this earlier stage of development as the depressive position, which epitomised for us the psychological development that was beginning to occur within the group. Copley and Forryan refer to this Kleinian concept as:

> Implicit in the achievement of the depressive position is the growth of a good object inside (no longer 'ideal' but merely 'good') that is felt to have sufficient strength to enable [the infant] to tolerate the absence of an external loved person and bear separations. It also implies taking responsibility for our relationship to other people and to our internal objects, facing the sadness for damage that we may have caused, bearing guilt and being willing to do what is within our capacity to put things right. If it is beyond our ability to put things right we need to be able to stand back and let others do so if they can . . . We also need to try and bear what cannot be restored without resorting to a denial of the damage. (Copley and Forryan, 1987)

One session in early summer illustrates their psychological development towards a group functioning. Peter, Louise, Tracey, Dean, and the two therapists were present, the remaining two young people were on a course. Peter bantered rivalrously with Louise; Louise spoke angrily about her family and the therapist letting her down over the cancellation of an appointment. She showed fury at Tracey, who chose not to sit beside her. Louise extended her work on a snake model making an ill-matched base (a container) and adding a 'daddy' snake and a 'baby' snake with modelling material. She threw white paint on the model family saying, 'a bird was pooing on them' (Figure 6.11). The group joined in her laughter and Peter began cutting his lino tile pattern into a snake shape, linking with Louise about angry feelings towards adults, particularly family.

Louise then spoke about her difficulties with her mother's current partner. Tracey received and contained Louise's feelings by sharing with her how hard it could be, but explaining how situations could change, relating to her own changed relationship with her mother's partner. Louise was able to put her earlier anger into perspective and responded in a way which showed she valued Tracey's perception. Dean and Tracey shared some issues of job applications and Dean allowed Tracey to help him form a letter to a local firm. At that point Peter's anxieties about independence and his perceived inadequacies surfaced. He showed his need for dependency through sharing his literacy difficulties with the educational therapist, asking her to write down the name of the biscuit we shared in the group so that he could have some between meetings. 'I search around the shelves but I can't find the name,' was his telling comment. It seemed to us that the others' developing independence had put him in touch with his needy child-self and fear of abandonment

Figure 6.11 Louise's 'Snake family'.

and separation and he regressed to the earlier therapist-orientated state.

After these interchanges Louise was able to speak directly of her worries about her cancer returning, following the hospitalisation of two friends. It seemed that this, perhaps, was the focus of her earlier rage in the room and made sense of her fear of not being 'held in mind' by her family and group 'family'. Peter identified with Louise, sharing his worries about having diabetes and being put on the disability register. Tracey shared her anxiety about an imminent gall bladder operation and the expected death of a friend's new baby.

All the group explored their feelings and could become linked in their perceived inadequacies, their hurt and damaged selves, which led to expressing their anger towards the adults whom they felt had let them down. Louise returned to a sculpture begun in earlier sessions where she had made a clay cat (single imagery – therapist-orientated stage) and then a cave for the cat (container). She placed these on a board and painted in a black shadowy figure (possibly unvoiced fears of cancer returning). In this session she painted over the black figure and added a group of white stick figures of parents and four children and two pets. This felt like a symbolic representation of her 'group family/learning' experience where her fears and anger were contained.

These interactions made the group seem at ease with each other. They shared their work and achievements in an open manner and then tidied up together and left, joining in adolescent laughter.

Figure 6.12 Louise's 'Cave, cat and family'.

In witnessing the group's use of art and learning processes to tackle and integrate a complexity of feelings, we considered their actions and responses concerning the tensions between development and regression. The notion is that each individual's developmental pathway within the security of the group derives from their sense of fusion within it. Through identification with a basic assumption, along with their regression to an earlier omnipotent dependent state, a great resistance to staying in touch with feelings and keeping to the reality of task arises. Once an action allows an experience of success, resistance diminishes and possibilities of new internal resources occur. In this particular session, by staying with the task of using materials for self-expression and learning, members experienced a sense of mastery over their conflicting emotions which then encouraged development of internal resources, the capacity for tolerance of frustration, enjoyment of peer relationships and acceptance of each others' opinions.

This group-centred adolescent stage of each young person's developmental journey signified a great maturational step in the life of the group. From this point on the youngsters were able to move with increased fluidity between their regressed dependent states and their new-found, more mature, group membership which embodied the functioning characteristic of adolescence.

Communication Through Transference, Counter-transference and Projection

Transference and counter-transference are psychoanalytic concepts that we viewed as crucial in understanding the emotional experience between ourselves and the group. Case (1994) explains that the strong feelings experienced by the therapist can be understood as symbols of primitive, non-verbal communications from the patient or client. Copley (1987) views this process as one of communication of intense feelings as a means of locating unwanted, unbearable feelings into the therapist. The therapist's response to these feelings from the patient are recognised as counter-transference, which Copley describes as a projective identification from the client which can feel extremely hostile and uncommunicative, belittling or confusing. A danger within the therapeutic relationship is for the therapist to unknowingly act out counter-transference feelings and return them to the client, becoming a transference figure for the client – for example, a punishing, over-protective, over-indulgent parent or a persecuting teacher. Good feelings may also be engendered in the therapist, i.e., feelings of being a good 'mother', which the therapist may find difficult to relinquish in order to stay with the therapeutic task of exploring good and bad feelings.

We developed an ability to voice our thoughts about the feelings that we received as projections from the group. Bion sees this capacity of the therapist to receive, consider and reflect back to the client an understanding of unwanted projected feelings, as providing an arena where relationships can develop and accrue meaning. After each session we explored these thoughts and their impact on our capacity to remain a functioning therapeutic couple. We also communicated aloud within the group our experience of the projections as they occurred. This seemed to us to be akin to a parental couple baffling over the needs of their infant in order to communicate understanding and the containment of anxiety. This process relates to Bion's theory (1962) of the development of the capacity to think, to be curious, and attentive, which is reliant upon an early infant experience of the parents' interest and understanding of the infant's needs. Bion calls this process 'maternal reverie'. Our 'reverie' together within the group seemed to enable the young people to become in touch with their emotions and to experience understanding and recognition of their unwanted projected feelings.

Case (1994) substantiates our experience of communication through the mechanism of projection by the young people. She describes how a child transfers on to the therapist and projects into the therapist: 'unconscious images of [its] internal parents; a fusion of impulses and feelings, fantasies and external experience' (Case, 1994).

These unconscious processes took place in the matrix of the group's interpersonal communication between themselves and us, by their creativity and learning experiences within the sessions, which inevitably aroused our own anxiety and defences. Our communication and awareness of each other's struggle and emotional experience within the group, helped us to prevent the disablement of our thinking by the overwhelming nature of the projected feelings received. Racker (1968) draws attention to the difficulty of looking at issues of counter-transference because they make us feel personally and professionally vulnerable. The trust we had in each other as co-therapists allowed us openly to discuss our experiences of the projections which facilitated a greater understanding of the youngsters' communication about their own experience.

Examples of the Transference and Counter-transference Experience

Dean brought in a GCSE comprehension passage concerning a boy's relationship with his parents and his move from primary to secondary school. He had chosen this passage out of a selection of comprehension pieces which appeared to us to immediately reflect his own previous experience of difficulty in making the transition from one school to another. The passage was also about the boy's fear of growing up and losing the security of his immediate and loving family. Dean carried a different experience about his family relationships and in tackling this piece of work, drew boxes around all the 'feeling' words and phrases in the composition, which split them off from the overall meaning of the passage. We saw this as Klein's paranoid/schizoid position, the defensive splitting against an underlying anxiety reflected in the task. He could understand and identify with the boy feeling betrayed by his parents, but could not make the link between the words and the meaning, or understand the mother's close feeling towards her son and her despairing attempt to help him through the transition. If Dean knew the meaning of the words he would have to know the meaning of his relationship with his mother and this was too terrifying for him to manage. We considered this to be an expression of transference through the learning task.

Perhaps in the same way that Dean felt disconnected from the feelings between the mother and the boy – a transference of his own feelings for his mother – so the educational therapist experienced feelings of helplessness, loss and confusion in communicating with Dean, and thus an inability to reach him or teach him. This sense of 'stuckness' in the therapist seemed to be Dean's projection of his internal sense of loss and his blocked thinking to knowing, which prevented him from making the necessary connections for understanding. His fear of an independent state, which for him represented abandonment, resulted in his need greedily to seek a dyadic relationship with the educational therapist, while refusing to be fed through the learning task.

The art therapist also experienced the separateness, the splitting and loss of contact with Dean and the other therapist. The comprehension passage indicated the mother's wish to help the boy make a secure transition by providing his favourite food. When the educational therapist wondered with Dean about this he angrily retorted, 'It's only food', denying the mother's nurturing capacity while at the same time greedily using the therapist and monopolising her within the group. It seemed that Dean had regressed to a state of dependency, feeling lost and angry with his parental figures. As a therapist couple we coped with the counter-transference feelings of being stuck and struggled to maintain an awareness of one another's position and relationship with the group.

We wondered aloud together about the difficulty Dean seemed to be having with his task and his separateness from the rest of the group that day, his need to split the therapist couple and what might be evoking this sense of separation and lack of contact. Dean's transference experience of abandonment was further heightened by the absence of two group members on that day. When we were able to process this, Dean began to make more connections to others in the group and think about the missing members and the feelings evoked in him by their absence.

Another powerful experience of transference and counter-transference occurred during Louise's first session at the group. She ignored the art therapist with whom she had previously worked individually, showing a keen interest in making links with the educational therapist, and Tracey's use of black paint. Subsequently Louise became absorbed in painting black mounds with a red cross on top of one of them (Figure 6.13). Once completed, Louise looked at her picture in silence, then finally said she didn't know what she had painted. As we witnessed her imagery, we became filled with feelings of loss, emptiness, and dread and felt that she was communicating this experience to us in the transference. In processing our feelings after the session we thought these transference communications might relate to Louise's feelings about her survival within the sibling group, and the loss of the dyadic relationship with the art therapist. We considered that her painting had put her in touch with feelings of loss of a maternal figure which engendered unconscious fears of the return of her cancer and possible death. The art therapist acknowledged her painful feelings of being a bad and abandoning 'mother' and expressed anxiety that she had made the wrong decision about Louise joining the group. We recognised Louise's fears and anxieties by acknowledging the powerful impact of the imagery on ourselves and were able to resist acting out our own anxiety as part of the experience of transference and counter-transference.

In subsequent sessions the art therapist was able to comment on Louise's difficulties in keeping a relationship with her in the group and her need for dependency with the therapist couple. Through her difficult transition period into the group, Louise continued to project and split her feelings leaving the art therapist with her unwanted emotions of rejection and jealousy, while idealising and over-valuing the educational therapist's relationship with her. About nine months into the group, Louise was able to acknowledge the difficulties this transition had aroused in her and wrote a 'Good-bye and thank you' card to the art therapist referring to her previous individual sessions.

These examples reflect the overwhelming feelings expressed by individuals in the group, particularly in the dependency therapist-centred stage. We noticed, through the transference, that where some individuals attempted growth through the exploration of new materials, learning and training activities, other individuals struggled to make similar

Figure 6.13 Louise's first picture in group.

attempts but became stuck in their work because of an emotional unreadiness for this developmental move. During one session when Louise was free painting and talking about the opportunity of a job, Simon started to free paint for the first time. He became unable to link the images in his work which became messy and fragmented (Figure 6.14); he froze, showed discomfort, and was unable to finish the picture. Sitting alongside Simon during this experience we felt paralysed; our emptiness and hopelessness reflected the feelings he transferred to us. While Louise was emotionally ready, in this session, to explore independence through her verbal and art communications, Simon's attempts to explore this notion for himself resulted in the powerful unconscious expression of his terror and sense of disintegration.

Our counter-transference experience was to feel an urgent need to rescue Simon from his hopeless, helpless state. We sustained the onslaught of these feelings, commented on his difficulty and thought, with him, what he might want to happen next, acknowledging his struggle and disappointment with his experimental effort. He chose to leave the picture unfinished, folded it, and stored it in his folder. However, in the following session, Simon began a complex, perspective drawing of the inside of a building with long corridors with doors opening from it. He began this drawing several times before settling into a final draft to which he devoted months of sessions. Our containment of his projected feelings enabled him to face his fears and anxieties and discover new internal resources demonstrated in this determination to produce an

Figure 6.14 Simon's 'Sea picture'.

integrated piece of work. During the evolvement of this drawing he began a new college course. He began to verbalise freely for the first time within the group, and express his fears of managing the written work expected of him.

Conclusion

We have tried to illustrate by glimpses into the life and work of a young people's group some of the therapeutic processes we engaged in as a therapist couple, by being receptive to the group's projections throughout their interactions, art-making and learning processes. Their many conflicting and painful emotions, we allowed ourselves to experience and endure, through the transference and counter-transference. It was essential to engender a feeling of security for the young people to know, acknowledge, and integrate their difficult life experiences. We endeavoured to promote their internal capacity for change by recognising their regression and progression within various developmental stages. Being given an opportunity for second-chance learning and by being provided with a working space, members of the 'group/family' gained a different experience. By accepting the therapeutic process within the life of the group they could contemplate embarking on a hitherto inaccessible, seemingly impossible journey of exploration towards adolescence and burgeoning independence.

Chapter 7
Educational Therapy and the Classroom Teacher

HEATHER GEDDES

Thinking with Teachers about Children's Emotional Difficulties and the Effects on their Learning in School

This chapter seeks to examine the contribution that educational therapy thinking can make to the teacher working in mainstream and special schools with children whose learning is affected by emotional and behavioural difficulties. Educational therapy with individual children in the setting of the Child Guidance Unit enables insights into the relationship between the pupils' learning difficulties, their behaviour and their relationship with the teacher. The insights derived are translatable into the classroom setting, helping to develop the teacher's awareness of their experience and perception of the difficulties that some pupils face.

The classroom teacher plays a significant role in the identification and support of pupils with special educational needs (SEN). Policies are changing, moving away from resourcing the individual child to a more preventative model based on Warnock's 'Stages of Intervention' (Warnock, 1978). These rely heavily on the teacher's response to the difficulties of the child. Such developments can represent a considerable pressure on the classroom teacher and the school as a whole. The class teacher is the person who experiences the unwanted behaviour most and at the same time is expected to react with concern and thoughtful interventions. A teacher can feel ambivalent about a pupil who is causing disruption. Interactions between the teacher and the pupil can be stressful and exacerbated by teachers working in isolation. Caspari (1976) wrote: 'exhaustion felt by most teachers at the end of term is more closely linked to the demands made on the skills and personality of a teacher in keeping discipline over the children than to any other aspect of the work'.

Pratt (1978) found children's behaviour among the most highly rated sources of stress for teachers in a survey of primary schools in Sheffield. Galloway et al. (1985) confirm this: 'children with special needs, whose behaviour and/or progress are almost by definition particularly disturbing to teachers, are a frequent source of stress in day-to-day classroom teaching'.

The question addressed in this chapter is whether the theory and practice of educational therapy can contribute to this situation and benefit the teacher and the child.

Who are the Children that Cause Concern?

The largest group of children, i.e., those who are not 'handicapped in the traditional sense of the term', but whose 'learning problems ... may last for varying periods of time' (Warnock, 1978), have emotional, social and behavioural difficulties (DES, 1982; Croll and Moses, 1985). In their Newcastle study, Kolvin et al. (1981) found that 25% of pupils aged between 7 and 8 years experienced emotional difficulties. These children can be dependent on the resources of schools for considerable periods of time, and teachers' experience is crucial in understanding such difficulties. But this may be clouded by stress, and it is necessary to examine how teachers' concerns are affected by children's behaviour.

The educational therapist believes that all behaviour has meaning. Experience of educational therapy with individual children suggests that emotional experience can directly affect a child's ability to think and to learn in very specific ways (Beaumont, 1991). The effects of a child's behaviour on the teacher and the nature of the child's difficulties are communications. A deeper understanding of these can lead to an appropriate response.

However, for the teacher of the child with emotional and behavioural difficulties this can be an obscure and puzzling process, a point at which the experiences of the teacher and the educational therapist converge. What the teacher experiences as puzzling, the therapist calls 'hard to think about'. The child's difficulties can seem incomprehensible in the class because the communication is obscure and often accompanied by behaviour that engages and provokes feelings and reactions in their teachers. For the child, the difficulties may represent unprocessed experiences. In the clinical setting and the accompanying supervision, the educational therapist has had time to reflect on unprocessed experiences and to think about the effects that such experience can have on a child's capacity to progress in school. When the educational therapist and the teacher think together, this experience of working with such children can be translated into the classroom and help to clarify the confusion that the teacher is experiencing.

In our different settings the process is very similar; how to make sense of our experiences and concerns so that a more effective educational response can be planned. The starting point is the interaction between the pupil and the teacher within which there is communication that has become obscured and difficult to understand. Examples from this collaborative work of thinking together are described later. It is important to look first at the possible meaning of the interactions between teachers and pupils.

What Might be Happening Between Teacher and Pupil in the Classroom?

Whether in the mainstream or the special class, adults and children can interact in ways that can cloud the issue of the teaching and learning processes. We can become aware of certain kinds of common behaviours that affect others. This behaviour can be quite unconscious on the part of the child but have a powerful impact on others. Certain aspects of behaviour recur which I will describe, because they have underpinned many discussions about children presenting difficulties in class.

The importance of these examples is not necessarily to analyse the unconscious motives of the children, it is an impossible task and potentially dangerous to assume meaning without information. One can bring an awareness of the possible meaning of behaviour so that teachers can defend themselves against being drawn into further confusion or confrontations that can be personally damaging and unfruitful. (Some aspects of interactions will be briefly discussed and later demonstrated by examples from teachers' work.)

Projecting painful feelings

Children come to school upset for many different reasons. When asked why they are upset they more or less let others know what bothers them and they can be comforted or reassured. Such children are able to convey what their feelings are. Problems can arise when children are not able to say what upsets them. Observation of their behaviour is an important communication about their difficulties. Without any apparent explanation children can hurt others' feelings by an abusive remark or by an aggressive act; or set others against each other, causing fights, arguments and disagreements while claiming *they* have been provoked; things are taken and others accused; or they may avoid any work and blame others for distracting them. Some lose everything that is given them to do and say someone else has taken it, or they may withdraw into inertia, make the teacher feel shut out and irrelevant and then accuse the teacher of taking no notice of them. The feature of this behaviour is that such children upset others but deny being upset themselves.

The painful feelings that cause such reactions may be too hard to bear and are split off into other people so that the other people become upset on their behalf. This is known as 'projection' and is a normal process which can be a useful tool in communicating difficult feelings. In infancy, distress is communicated by crying. Crying babies are very hard to ignore and can upset adults around them. In this way the baby communicates its distress very effectively to the mother or other attachment figure and the baby relies on the emotional availability and sensitivity of an adult who can contain such unbearable feelings.

Feelings of failure

No matter how much positive verbal reward and encouragement are used, there are always some children who continue to have a sense of being no good or not good enough. This is expressed by acting out their feelings of being no good by trashing their work, losing it, storing it in a messy and careless way, or allowing it to be torn and scribbled on. It can show in presenting a pathetic appearance, unkempt and dishevelled as if they felt like rubbish themselves. Their own feeling of being useless may be denied and projected into others and they can then say how stupid others are or how useless their work is and be endlessly critical of other children's efforts. Some children need an omnipotent defence of believing that they know everything and that the teacher can't teach them anything, a defence against their own vulnerability and sense of stupidity. This is particularly damaging as it is not possible to learn if you cannot accept not knowing. Omnipotence is a common symptom among children referred to the clinic for educational therapy as it often accompanies children whose learning is seriously stuck. The class teacher can experience children's omnipotence as feeling deskilled and useless themselves.

The Importance of Communication

Children often experience difficult relationships at home where adults disagree or are in damaging conflict, leaving a child feeling disloyal to both members of a warring couple or trapped between them, either to prevent the conflict, preserve the partnership or to protect a parent from harm. There are many reasons for children to assume this powerful position in a family and their preoccupation can leave them with little time for being a child or for the concerns of the classroom. This ability to be 'in between' and to split relationships can be seen in children who are always falling in and out of the triangular friendship, children who find it hard to work in a group without taking control or causing others to fall out, children who tell adults different stories so that colleagues can find themselves in opposition, believing different versions of an incident.

This ability to split relationships is particularly damaging if communication problems exist between, for example, support staff and teaching staff.

The implication is that adults need to be aware of the importance of clear and collaborative communication. Consistent and open explanation and shared thinking can help to model and foster an experience that communication is a fruitful process, rather than one fraught with danger and confusion. Where adults demonstrate the ability to communicate effectively about disagreement and take responsibility for resolving difficulties without the intervention of children, then the child is free to go about his or her own business of being a child.

Relationships

In the classroom learning takes place within the relationship of each pupil and teacher, the class group and teacher, and between the pupils themselves. In many ways these relationships reflect some experience of previous relationships at home, principally the one between mother and infant (although also with siblings). In order to learn effectively, the pupil must be able to trust the teacher, assume that what they say is truthful (which is not the same as always right), want to please them and mind enough about their disapproval to want to try harder. Similarly the child needs to be able to trust the adult enough to believe that their criticism or disapproval is an expression of their concern for them and not a sadistic need to be cruel and punitive.

However, children can bring to the relationship with the teacher some of the negative expectations that they have learned in the parental relationship, or they may have the ability to turn the teacher into the parent they are used to, such as by repeatedly behaving in ways that elicit negative responses. The child may not be happiest in this negative relationship but it is the mode of behaviour that is most familiar and easiest to maintain. The desired result of constant teacher attention, even though negative attention, may still be better than feeling ignored and unnoticed.

Family relationships are inevitably re-enacted in the classroom. Sibling rivalries are demonstrated as children vie for the attention of the teacher or compete for meagre resources. Twins can experience particular difficulties (chapter 3). Mealtimes can be a reminder of infantile anxieties. Temper and rages enacted on ancillary staff can indicate previous tensions. Very clear procedures help to reduce some of the strong feelings experienced at times when family life is most evoked.

Separations and Endings

School life begins with a significant experience of separation and more than any other time the child re-enacts earlier experiences of separation from the parent and family. Successive transitions then occur throughout school life. Each one reflects the earlier experience and is a chance to reprocess the experience of separation more successfully. Rituals of beginning and ending of the day, term and year, build gradually towards the transition to secondary school and ultimately from school and from family. Where endings are ignored or denied then unresolved feelings can remain, for example they can be marked by vandalism and acts of angry rejection. It is not uncommon for supply teachers who take over a class to suffer much rejection and anger, by a class who perceives itself as rejected, unless it can be convinced that the teacher intends to stay for the stated period.

Transition to secondary school is challenging to all pupils and at best can be a mixture of excited anticipation tinged with anxieties about being able to cope. But for some it is an overwhelming reminder of the uncertainty created by numerous changes of teachers and schools. The form tutor for the early years in secondary school has a particularly important role to play at this time.

The Relationship between Pupil and Teacher

The nature of a child's attachment to the parent is a significant factor in their capacity to learn in school. Attachment theory proposes that the infant–mother relationship is the secure base from which the child is able to venture and explore and derive the inner strength with which to face challenges and disappointments without damage or too much distress. The quality of this early relationship can vary enormously and an understanding of this can be very helpful to the teacher in thinking about and acknowledging some of the known difficulties that can undermine some children.

The teacher's relationship with a pupil is very important in the learning process and there will always be echoes of the early maternal relationship. For most this will have been a good enough experience and have provided them with a sufficiently secure base from which to learn and develop socially. For others it may be difficult for the teacher to establish a relationship which is supportive and dependable but does not foster unnecessary dependence. The difference between the therapist and the teacher is most marked in this respect in that the therapist does work with transference feelings whereby the child may attach maternal significance to the relationship. In this way the child is helped to develop a stronger internalised base from which he or she may have a second chance to begin to learn.

The child may bring this need for a maternal attachment to school but the unambiguous role of the teacher is paramount. For such a child it is more helpful to experience an appropriate relationship with clear boundaries and expectations than to have a confusing one repeated. It can take time for this new relationship to become established and for a while small children can be heard calling the teacher 'mum' and teachers can feel an inappropriate concern for some pupils. A child's anger and ambivalence towards their parent can be projected on to a teacher but is a clue about the child's difficulties rather than a true reflection of their feelings towards the teacher.

Collaboration with Parents

The educational therapist working in the multi-disciplinary setting has the support of colleagues and can establish a collaborative network of parents, child and school (Dowling and Osborne, 1994). Within this, adults share their concerns which empowers the parents and allows their children to see them working cooperatively with teachers. This is a particularly potent experience for children, enabling them to experience a safe and contained framework within which they can be free of their disabling anxieties and begin to think and to learn. It cannot be over-emphasised that the collaboration and shared thinking between the school and the parents is the most helpful framework to the child's ability to learn effectively in school.

Many children now live in single-parent families or in reconstituted families. This remains the private concern of the parents but 'The Exeter Family Study' (Cockett and Tripp, 1994) research indicates that for a significant number of children this is challenging and results in under-achievement in school.

Limits and Boundaries

Areas of difficulty repeatedly discussed with me by teachers, are the effect on them of pupil behaviour, the setting of boundaries and the role of sanctions. These have particular meaning for the experience of learning and are the single most important factors in school life that can establish and maintain an environment within which thinking can take place.

Rules are more than a social convenience and have greater significance. Limits set, and kept, by caring adults imply a concern for children's welfare and a determination to maintain a safe environment. If they gain confidence in the adults' ability to maintain a safe and secure situation they become free enough of anxieties to attend to school events and the challenges of learning. Some level of uncertainty and anxiety are normal: they are part of the experience of successfully overcoming frustrations and challenges, which themselves are part of the learning process. But too much anxiety can be overwhelming and severe anxiety or trauma can be disabling to the thinking process.

Many children who come to school have experienced stress and sometimes trauma. This can result in children functioning with a constant and preoccupying level of anxiety that undermines their ability to focus on tasks and to think. The setting and keeping of limits by concerted adult agreement and persistence, are fundamental in minimising the levels of anxiety of staff or pupils. When children are not certain of the intentions of the adults they may persist in challenging the adults until safety is assured.

Because of the fundamental importance of this basic requirement for safety and containment, schools may react and become heavily sanctioned. It is as if they are not confident of their ability to maintain safety, and resort to extreme control. Such systems can be experienced as abusive and provoke the very anxieties that are the underlying problem. The message that is implicit in very controlling regimes is that the adults are not confident of their ability to maintain safety. They may feel threatened by overwhelming feelings projected by children with high levels of anxiety. The balance between containment and control is a sensitive one which requires careful and collaborative planning of a positive policy towards limits and sanctions. The school which successfully combines limits and sanctions is operating a therapeutic ethos which is reassuring to both pupils and teachers and conducive to higher levels of thinking and learning.

The Importance of Awareness of Unconscious Processes

These interactions and needs, often of an unconscious nature, can be present in any classroom and can have a greater or lesser effect on the teacher and the pupils. However they are potentially disruptive and damaging and an awareness of them can diminish stress to the teacher. When the teacher understands the nature of an interactive processes this can inform them about the child's emotional and behavioural difficulties and leads to an appropriate response – not in order to become a therapist but to be more effective as a teacher.

By developing self-awareness and thinking about the interactive behaviour of others, most reactions to unconscious communications are better understood. The experiences and perceptions of both the pupil and the teacher which are brought to every learning–teaching relationship are unique. The context within which this happens is particularly significant. Whole school practices play a large part in establishing the ethos within which the pupil-teacher interaction takes place.

Clearly, some schools reflect a more therapeutic ethos than others. In my experience schools need to develop therapeutic practices because they enhance emotional, cognitive and professional development: this applies to all schools whether mainstream or special. Therapeutic thinking benefits all pupils while benefiting the neediest most.

Examples of the Application of Therapeutic Thinking in Classrooms

It is my experience in working with groups of teachers responsible for children with emotional and behavioural difficulties that they all have the necessary skills but often have become deskilled by the unconscious processes and interactions that have been described. In the past this work was then referred to other 'experts' but with such resources now shrinking, teachers are having to develop their own 'special needs' skills and ways of working more effectively within the context of their classrooms. Teachers working in isolation are particularly vulnerable: training that enables collaboration is therefore preferable, providing teachers with opportunities to share experiences as well as expertise, develop comparable skills and update policies. The support of colleagues has been reported by teachers as the most fruitful aspect of working together.

The model upon which collaborative work can be based is the 'consultation workshop' developed and described by Hanko (1985, 1990). This is a framework within which difficult issues can be explored by colleagues in a mutually supportive way. The structure of the workshops is a group with a facilitator who structures the beginning and the end of the session and facilitates thinking and reflection about the meaning of the difficulties described. Within the agreed boundaries of time and confidentiality and mutual respect, each member presents a problem. The content of the presentation is then discussed and thought about by colleagues with the facilitator.

In such a setting the following examples are reported with sufficient changes to preserve anonymity, and serve to demonstrate the use of supportive group work, as well as the therapeutic value of shared thinking and reflection, in bringing about change. Solutions and strategies proposed and developed were almost always within the resources of the classroom or the school and during the course of the work teachers made fewer references to outside agencies and other 'experts' (Geddes, 1991).

'Boys that make me angry'

A class teacher in a primary school discussed her class of 9/10-year-olds. In the class, no matter how she felt when she came to work, as soon as a particular group of boys walked into the classroom, she felt angry with them and remained embattled with them all day. Everything they did annoyed her. She described them as a group who tried to take over the class and undermine her authority. She was upset because she felt she was not herself, unable to control her feelings and unable to get on with the job of teaching the class.

Her anger seemed to be stopping her from thinking about ways of dealing effectively with the boys' apparent need for power and dominance. In the discussion of the presentation it was suggested that one of the boys, or the group, brought their anger from elsewhere into the class and projected it on to her. When the teacher recognised this possibility she was able to step back and begin to think about how the boys might be feeling. Was their preoccupation with feelings from outside school affecting their ability to think about what was expected of them within the class?

She was able see that she had been experiencing their anger and not her own. Being able to distance herself from their projected feelings she could think again as the teacher. Ways were found to channel the boys' feelings by drama activities which enabled the safe expression of hostility in roles and parts. Within the class, responsibilities were delegated that enabled the boys to experience appropriate power 'but with responsibility' within the peer group.

The teacher later reported that she felt relieved to be able to disentangle her feelings from those of the group of boys and to see them more clearly as pupils with difficulties. She made opportunities within the curriculum to help with these difficulties and the boys functioned better socially and had less effect on others in the class. She felt more effective, personally and professionally. An explanation of this situation might be that the boys were experiencing feeling small and insignificant elsewhere. These are painful feelings that were not thought about but brought to school and projected into the teacher as anger and acted out on the class as inappropriate seeking for power and control in order to restore feelings of importance. The teacher was available for the projected anger for reasons of her own and became enmeshed in the unconscious processes and was unable to think clearly about the issues or resources available.

'A class that doesn't do what I want them to'

A music teacher who saw a class of top infants twice a week for singing and music found the group very difficult and tended blame four children in the class who were described as very disruptive. As the class began the work planned, the disruption began and she would generally have to abandon the song in order to stave off the disruption. This resulted in the teacher feeling that the class would not cover the National Curriculum requirements, leaving her feeling very undermined and deskilled by the lack of success with this class. She struggled to describe this to her colleagues because of her feelings of failure.

The class teacher was supposed to be present in the music lessons but had been very busy with Standard Attainment Tests (SATs). This absence was agreed, leaving the music teacher feeling like a babysitter, a feeling reinforced by the class's infantile behaviour, thumb-sucking and snuggling up to the teacher when she was present. The class had enjoyed a lesson when they played an instrument but, when she tried to repeat the lesson, the disruptions soon began again and she abandoned the attempt. In another successful lesson the class had acted a song with parts. The teacher reported that the children, especially the timid ones, seemed more able to sustain effort when playing parts.

As this situation was discussed, the teacher began to lose her sense of despondency and frustration and to think with her colleagues about how the children might be experiencing the lesson. They thought about the confusion of not knowing when their class teacher would be present and the lack of explanation for her absence. It was pointed out that singing was a challenging thing to do, and required self-confidence. It was thought that the teacher's lack of persistence may have left the children feeling inappropriately powerful and unsure. These issues were discussed and strategies proposed, including returning to the original lesson plan and the unfinished songs, plus arranging for the class teacher to begin and end the lesson and to tell them where she would be otherwise. More lessons were planned to incorporate work in the metaphor, for example songs about soldiers, and the use of objects and masks. The music teacher later reported having several successful lessons with the class. Some parents told her of their child's interest in a particular song by talking about it in church. The class teacher reported that the class had told others that they were good at playing musical instruments. Although the class could revert to 'babyish' behaviour at times and vie for the class teacher's attention, this behaviour no longer dominated the lesson and the 'disruptive' children were not seen as the source of difficulty.

On reflection, the group with whom this work was discussed thought that the class may have been too dependent on their class teacher and unexplained separations from her may have made them feel uncertain and anxious. This made it hard for them to accept the 'other' teacher, and to concentrate on the musical tasks, until they were given an explanation for their teacher's absences and reunions were arranged. Then the class was able to sustain the separation and think about the music lesson. This example highlights two other factors; that working in the metaphor is a very valuable form of engaging pupils in emotive issues which involve strong feelings, and, because the class teacher and the music teacher were working together in the staff group, they were able to recognise the part they both played in bringing about the situation and could collaborate in its resolution.

Acknowledging feelings

A teacher in a special school had a boy in his class who was always upset and angry. Everything that happened left him in a bad temper. Eventually, the normally patient teacher became angry and resorted to severe sanctions to control and minimise the disturbance to the rest of the class. He described the aspects of the boy's life that may well have caused him to be confused and frustrated and to feel helpless and angry. The group began to understand the level of frustration that could overwhelm the boy. This helped the teacher to distance himself from the projections of anger and to think instead about the boy's feelings. Later, when the boy came in, in his usual angry state, complaining that something unfair had happened in the playground, his teacher reacted differently. He remained calm and said to the boy that he understood how unfair things sometimes felt, how frustrating that must be, and how awful that could feel. The teacher describes the boy as changing before his eyes, becoming calmer and able to walk to his place and get on with some work. This teacher reflected that he had been able to make the boy feel understood, even though he could not affect the issues that were the cause of the difficulties. Communicating understanding, whether to the stressed teacher or to the distressed child, can enable sufficient reduction in anxiety to allow thinking to take place.

Using the metaphor

A support teacher was working in a secondary school class with a boy described as 'aged 13 years, very withdrawn, with limited basic skills and who just can't get started'. The teacher introduced a particular series of reading books with the harder text on one side of the pages and easier text on the other. The book was called *When the clock struck 13*. The story is about an iron boy who is the striking mechanism of a clock. One night the boy strikes 13 by mistake and something magical happens. He finds that he can move and climbs down from the tower and into a magician's room. He tells the magician that he wants to be free and to grow up like other boys. The magician discourages him saying the world is a difficult place. The boy is determined to be free, so the magician tells him he will have to go on a long and difficult journey to find, and cross, the Silver River. The boy decides to go despite the magician's warnings.

The next book of the series, *The Sandalwood Girl*, is about a doll who has sat on the shelf, neglected and forgotten, and is similarly freed by the 13 strikes of the clock. She also meets the magician and receives the same advice and makes the same decision. The iron boy and the wooden girl set off together to find the Silver River. They have adventures along the way and they meet characters who advise them but do not actually do things for them. They eventually achieve what they wish for and become real.

The boy worked very hard to read the easier text but soon wanted to read the harder text and laboured to do so despite the difficulties. He persisted until he succeeded. As the boy struggled with the task of reading the story, with its content concerning taking risks and not turning back, the discussion with the teacher clearly mirrored the experience of the boy as he tackled the challenging task of reading. Alongside this, the teacher worked with written material, sentences from the story that had to be put in correct sequence, and a board game devised to accompany the story.

This teacher recognised similar difficulties in other boys of that age and uses the series with them to support and help them overcome much of the despondency that stems from an absence of earlier support. It held a message of conviction that they will begin the process of learning. This is particularly relevant during the passage from childhood to adolescence.

There are many stories for children that have wonderful potential for making use of metaphors and the safe discussion of difficult issues. It is not always necessary to confront emotional issues head on, as many can be explored, and thought about, in a variety of ways.

Summary

The examples described above are of problems experienced by teachers working in a range of educational settings. The difficulties arose when their professional capacity was affected by children's behaviour and associated interactions. When children consciously or unconsciously adopt unacceptable behaviour as a means of communicating their difficulties, learning or social, teachers become concerned but find it difficult to re-evaluate objectively. Problems can be hard to assess and so an appropriate response may be difficult to develop.

The teacher's ability to think is affected in the same way as the child's, by emotional issues that need to be processed. Educational therapy in the clinic setting can restore the child's capacity to think. In a similar way, the teacher's capacity to think about the child's difficulties can be restored by an applied process of reflection in a setting that is facilitating. The outcome of applying educational therapy thinking to the teacher's experience is to reduce stress, enhance teaching skills by responding differently to the child's educational needs, through developing an understanding of emotional factors, and making less use of outside agencies.

This is true for mainstream and special schools. However, for the special school teacher, the experience of individual need can be intensified and the learning issues become even more obscure and entrenched.

Collaborative thinking then seems essential in order to address the emotional issues that are affecting most of the children working with the teacher. In this setting it may be necessary for collaboration to take on the nature of individual supervision, as practised by clinically trained educational therapists, social workers or psychotherapists.

Conclusion

A teacher's capacity to think can be restored by the reflective process fundamental to the therapeutic process. This does not imply a change in the teacher's role but a reinforcement of it. The content of any curriculum in any school can be better understood and accomplished if communication can be enhanced by the use of the metaphor.

In order to introduce these therapeutic qualities that enhance learning, the context within which such understanding develops is of great significance and the practices that a school develops and adopts can help to enhance a therapeutic ethos. In particular, the policy on rules and sanctions can be indicative of policy aimed at protecting the pupils and the teachers from excessive anxiety and so benefit the learning process.

The importance of remaining the teacher is paramount. Concern for a child's intellectual development is equal to concern about emotional development; they are interrelated. In this respect the needs of schools to acknowledge the importance of emotional factors in learning, and for this to be reflected in their whole school practices, is probably the biggest single contribution to the ethos of the school. In this sense the practice of educational therapy and classroom practice are the same: recognition and concern for the role of emotional factors in any child's learning experiences.

Chapter 8
Holding on to the Unbearable

MARGARET STOKES

An Attempt to Interact with an Angry, Hostile, Six-year-old

As a part of the Diploma course in Educational Therapy Techniques, I was required to carry out a detailed piece of interaction with a child who I considered might benefit from the experience, and who would provide me with material for group supervision.

I had a considerable choice of subjects, since I work with a small class of children, all of whom have emotional and behavioural difficulties (E.B.D.). The overall ethos of the school is of a behaviourist nature, with emphasis on delivery of the National Curriculum, and academic achievement, rather than in any in-depth consideration of the reasons behind a child's disturbing behaviour. With positive reinforcement, strong and firm boundaries set, good behaviour modelled and practised and, above all, a good pupil–teacher ratio, it could be said that the children improved and developed. Nevertheless, I felt that if these children were to manage themselves in often extremely difficult environments, outside the classroom, greater insight into their experiences on my part might benefit them.

Melanie

For the purpose of my diploma study, I decided to work with Melanie, the only girl in the class. Although I have focused mainly on my individual work with her, to emphasise her unpredictable and mercurial behaviour, this experience helped me to understand her behaviour, and that of the other children, more constructively, in the day-to-day classroom interactions. Melanie is six years old and lives in a small block of flats, in a fairly poor but settled city area. The family consists of Mr and Mrs Clayson and their three children, Sam (8), Melanie (6) and Lisa (3). Mr Clayson has another family of two young children living in the same city.

There appear to be occasional meetings of the two families Melanie refers to them as 'cousins'.

Melanie's father

Mr Clayson is a large man, an ex-boxer who has worked as a bouncer in local night clubs, and is occasionally employed on local fairgrounds. He is known as an alcoholic, although reported to be 'dried out' now, and has been addicted to drugs and also convicted for dealing. He admits that his children have suffered emotional and physical abuse in their early years, as a result of his behaviour, but claims he is now trying to make amends for his past offences. His size, his 'tough' appearance and his body posture can make his presence in a room feel quite threatening. When he has come into school, Melanie has approached him with obvious mixed feelings. She shrieks as if in fear, sobs loudly with tears running down her cheeks, yet runs towards him, arms wide, shouting, 'Daddy, my daddy.' She is a fragile-looking child, and when picked up by her father, he must appear huge to her as she is hugged very close. To the onlooker, it is obvious that he has great physical power over this little girl, who appears extremely vulnerable. I think the anxiety felt by Melanie at these times must be considerable.

Melanie's mother

Mrs Clayson has only been into school on one occasion. She is an average-sized woman, tidily dressed, who sat impassively while her husband spoke. She seemed content to let him do all the talking, but did not appear cowed or overawed by the situation, or by the demeanour of Mr Clayson. She gave the impression of not caring, of being rather bored, of just waiting until the meeting was over. When it was suggested that Melanie might have been sexually abused, her face barely registered any change in its passivity.

Schooling

Melanie began her schooling in a mainstream school which her brother also attended. Both children were referred to the Schools Psychological Service because of the behavioural problems they presented in school. A statement of Special Educational Needs (S.E.N.) was drawn up for Melanie, recommending placement in an E.B.D. school where her problems could be better addressed and her behaviour more successfully managed.

I had visited her as her prospective class teacher, in her mainstream class. The greatest concern expressed by the head and class teachers, was for her own safety, and for that of the other children around her.

Melanie could not be persuaded to remain in her classroom, let alone on her chair, and spent much of the day rushing up and down a long corridor outside the classroom, shrieking and shouting obscenities. If pursued, she would run out of school and taunt the staff with gestures and a 'can't catch me' pose. She ran across roads, jumped on top of parked cars, and generally showed no regard for her own safety, or the property of others. The staff at the school reported considerable aggravation from Melanie's parents, particularly her father, and did not seem optimistic about the future of the children within the family. They did not suspect that any sexual abuse might have occurred.

The Family in the Community

Melanie's family is well known within the local community for its chaotic and anti-social lifestyle. Both Sam and Melanie have reputations for bullying and threatening, particularly of elderly people. Melanie will kick on doors until they are opened, and will refuse to leave until she is given whatever she has demanded. She will actually enter houses through windows, and 'menace' the elderly occupants, who are afraid to deal with such a young girl, or to complain to her parents. She has been doing this since she was four years old. If anyone tries to stop her, she will kick them and shout in foul and abusive language. She is not welcome in the local shops because of her threatening behaviour and her shoplifting of small items.

Melanie in an E.B.D. Setting

Having been in the classroom with Melanie for more than a year, there is one description of her which constantly recurs in my mind; she is 'foul-mouthed'. Not only is her conversation full of obscenities and swear words, she will eat anything from the ground, put inedible objects in her mouth, spit, gag, cough as if to vomit or belch. Her teeth are decaying and her breath foul smelling, and she frequently screams and wails. Melanie often presents herself in the classroom as one of the adults. She imitates adult behaviour and conversation, and gives instructions to other children, as if she were their somewhat downtrodden and harassed mother. In her play in the home corner, she can be heard berating, and verbally abusing, an imaginary husband or neighbours, using expressions such as, 'Who do you think you are?'; 'Well, you can forget that!'

Paradoxically, there are many things that Melanie cannot forget. I see these expressions as significant in their frequency. Melanie does not know who she is, child or adult. Her role of mother in a play situation always ends up in violence, with the 'baby' being screamed at and flung violently against the wall. At other times she will be the baby demanding to be fed, then 'winded' and patted. This play results in a theatrical vomiting of the 'food' all over the 'mother'.

In a newspaper article, Susie Orbach (1993) states: 'Each person brings their history to the present. We make and shape present relationships with reference to past experiences, and anticipate acceptance or rejection based on an emotional knowledge of what has gone before.' She goes on to say of a mother, 'It is in her arms, with her words, her food, her emotional ambience that we are introduced to the world. At first . . . she *is* our world. We apprehend its shape, the way things are and how things feel through her presence. She is embedded in our very sense of self. We become individual human beings by imbibing who she is inside us.'

John Bowlby (1988) points out the importance of libidinal relationships (a Freudian term): 'In high degree indeed, a person's whole emotional life – the underlying tone of how he feels – is determined by the state of these long-term, committed relationships.' Linnet McMahon (1992) writes of children who, like Melanie, have experienced conflict, neglect and abuse in the first two years of their life, presenting very deep-seated problems: 'Many of these children will have experienced adults who are indifferent, resentful, jealous, angry and violent, intermittently throughout their lives. They often identify with these adults and in turn display these attitudes in their relationships with others, covering up their pain by projecting their feelings.' She continues, 'Therefore the best clue to how these children are really feeling lies in how they make the worker feel, whether it is useless, no good, wiped out or annihilated, helpless or "bad".'

Melanie certainly portrays herself as very mixed up about her own identity. She presents as both an adult, full of abuse, aggression and omnipotence, and as an infant wanting to be carried, fed from a bottle and utterly vulnerable. Irene Caspari (1974) refers to the importance of 'feeding' in the development towards healthy emotional and academic progress:

> It is generally accepted that successful feeding of infants depends not only on the interaction between the mother and the child, but also on the appropriateness of the food and the manner in which it is given. Similarly, in the learning situation the interaction of the teacher and his pupil, the degree to which the teaching material is gauged to the pupil's appetite and whether or not it is presented so that he can take it in.

Melanie rarely eats with the family at home, her mother reported. 'She just "picks" at food, whenever she feels like it.' In school, she sits around a 'family' table and readily conforms to the social 'rules' of family eating. It would seem as if no one cares sufficiently about Melanie to make her do as she is told within her home. She is allowed to break any rules that might be imposed, as do all the other members of the family, whenever they do not choose to conform. Melanie is shouted at with foul language and returns with the same. Since she has been in her present class, Melanie has been spoken to with respect as a worthwhile person, and as a child who needs to be guided and kept safe. Since she has not been sworn at or verbally abused over a period of time, an improvement in her relationships within the classroom is very apparent. I found the 'educational attachment figure', an important concept by Barrett and Trevitt (1991), relevant in my work with Melanie. This is the development, within a professional boundary, of an attachment between the child and the teacher/therapist. Before Melanie could begin any 'second-chance learning', another concept by these authors, her need to form an attachment is evident in her closeness to the adults within the classroom, as is her need to regress into infancy. It is difficult to imagine that Melanie and her mother ever formed a secure attachment. Indeed, it might be true that a negative and hateful relationship developed between them.

Working with Melanie

I withdrew Melanie from the group for seven one-hour sessions, over a period of eight weeks (with a break at mid-term). The sessions were difficult to organise and control. The actual space and time were not ideal. Within the known and defined boundaries of the classroom, there is an element of safety with the child knowing where the limits are at all times. In the area we used for our sessions people sometimes passed through, as there was open access to other rooms. However, this was the only possibility of maintaining a one-to-one situation, without interruption from other members of the class, and so we just had to manage.

In the introductory session I explained to Melanie what we were going to do. I emphasised that this time was just for her, that I hoped we would not be interrupted, and that I would tell her when it was five minutes until the end of the session. I took a lidded box and together we looked through the contents. The box contained paper, pencils, crayons, felt tips, cotton wool, scissors, plasters, ruler, sharpener, glue, tape, string, toy animals, doll's furniture and small dolls, simple story books, picture books, a magic wand, play dough, a miniature book, a tiny screwdriver, elastic bands and an eraser. I explained to Melanie that she could put the lid on her box at the end of our time and that it would be kept safe and unopened until next week.

In the first session, I asked Melanie to draw a picture of a man or a woman with as much detail as possible. She did this very hurriedly with little attention paid to what she was doing. When I pressed for more detail she added, talking all the time: 'There are . . . arms . . . and . . . legs . . .

and belly button.' She then decided to add Blu-tack to the belly button, colour the eyes red and put cotton-wool over the mouth. I wondered if she felt mouths held secrets or needed protection from something. Throughout all of my work with Melanie, both in and out of the classroom, her mouth plays a very significant role. During this session Melanie also played with the tiny book, nursery rhyme cards, doll's furniture, toy animals, play dough, screwdriver, plasters, story books, magic wand, crayons, and together we played the 'squiggle game' (Winnicott, 1971).

There were three incidents at this time. When playing with the play dough, Melanie was squeezing it in her fingers making 'urgh' sounds of revulsion. She did not attempt to make anything with the dough but said to herself, 'Oh! Disgusting little disgrace,' and began stabbing at it with the small screwdriver. Later, when playing with the magic wand, I asked her what spell she would like to make. She responded, again almost to herself, 'Make it. . . make the room into teeth.' Towards the end of the session, I asked her to draw her family, using a pencil first. She took about five seconds to do each of four people and said they were, 'Dad, Mummy, Sam and Lisa.' I asked Melanie if that was everyone in her family. 'Yes!' she replied emphatically and then added a figure at the end of the page and wrote her own name large and aggressively. She later coloured in the drawings, covering Dad's and Sam's faces particularly fiercely.

Dad   Mummy Sam Dora   Melanie.

Figure 8.1 Melanie.

In another session Melanie chose a hedgehog but was unable to name it and so took other things. She looked at the tape recorder and asked to have music on so she could sing. I said, 'No', and she started humming. She asked for some yellow tape to go round her crayon box and while trying to undo this tape she took my pen from my top pocket. I asked her to return it and she replied, 'Certainly' but removed the top and dabbed the tip into a tissue. She returned it and said, 'That looks like blood'. She asked for help in unwinding the tape and putting it round the crayon box, but I said, ' I think you manage that'. She tried for about 30 seconds and I offered her a pair of scissors to cut the tape. 'They might help,' she said. I repeated that I thought she could do it without my help and eventually she succeeded. Quite a lot of tape was used – more than necessary for the purpose – and she asked me if she would get more when it was all gone.

We were interrupted and Melanie was asked what she was doing. 'Just making a funny thing of sticky tape so it doesn't bite. So can you wait till I've finished?' she said. The visitor asked me about the programme I was following with Melanie, who replied for me, 'Certainly, yes'. I managed to get the visitor to leave, with Melanie shouting, 'Bye, bye!'

I asked Melanie to sit down twice, and suggested that while that she kept picking things up, taking the tops off pens, and generally fiddling she seemed unable to settle for long enough to enjoy the activity. She replied that she needed the pen to draw a picture: 'And I need some tape for its eyes, its belly button and its legs'. She very quickly drew a circle shape (head) but then immediately changed the activity by saying that she was doing a 'squiggle' which she passed to me. This felt very much as if Melanie was trying to take the adult role, as if she was trying to be me. I asked her to sit and explained again that we were going to do one thing at a time, and that if she wanted to play the squiggle game in a minute then we would. She agreed: 'Yes. Not for its eyes, I'm not using tape', she replied as she quickly added a body, two eyes and two arms. 'There, Mrs Stokes, but I'm not doing legs.'

'You did that well, didn't you, Melanie?' I commented. There was no response. 'Is that enough?'

'Bit too much,' Melanie muttered, taking some tape off the reel. She tried to stick it to the top of the figure she had drawn, saying it was hair. 'Mrs Stokes, what day is it?'

Together we decided it was Tuesday. She asked for help in cutting the tape, but before help could be given, she ripped it. It stuck to her fingers and she was quiet for 20 seconds, which seemed like a long time. She muttered something indecipherable and was then quiet for another minute, quietly saying to herself, 'What do you think you are doing?' and then uttering an inane shriek. I reminded her to be careful with the scissors. She asked if there would be any more tape when she had used all the reel up. I said that I did not have any more. 'Well I won't be using it then!' and she stuck some of the extravagantly unrolled tape back on to the reel.

Melanie then asked if she would still be at the same school at Christmas, and I had to tell her that I thought she would be, but that it was not just my decision. I commented that she seems to be happy in this school but there was no response to this.

After a brief pause: 'Mrs Stokes, this is totally stupid.' She banged a glue stick down and giggled in an uncomfortably forced manner. I commented that it did not sound like a real laugh and she tried a variation, even more forced, and said, 'How about that?' I remarked that it was very difficult to make a pretend laugh sound real, to which there was no response.

Melanie dropped the glue top and feigned surprise. She then tried to glue cotton wool on to her picture (accompanied by more laughter) resulting in lots of glue all over her fingers, the picture and the cotton wool. I asked if she minded. 'Yes, I do mind it. I want it off!' She tried to wipe her fingers on the wall, then continued to spread the glue, getting it all over her hands. She then asked if she would get any more cotton wool after she had used all there was and I replied, 'No, only what is in the box.' Melanie belched. 'Pardon.' She started singing 'da dee da' while putting glue and cotton wool on her picture, banging the glue very loudly. She then tried to start a conversation about something discussed by me and my classroom assistant earlier in the day. She asked if she could use my pen to do the nose and mouth. Together, we looked for something suitable in her box but on not finding anything I said she could use my pen. She put in tiny nostrils and then scribbled hard across the top of the head. Melanie added what I think were legs and coloured in the arms.

I suggested that Melanie put the things away in her box so that we could do something together. I asked her to sit on the chair. She was finding it very hard to keep still and, even while sitting, was extremely fidgety on the chair. I asked her if she was ready and she replied that she was. At this point, I noticed that she was chewing something, and realised that in her time off the chair, she had leaned against a painting easel belonging to another class, and had chewed off some old orange paint.

MS   'What have you got in your mouth, Melanie?' I had to repeat this.
Mel.   'My red tongue.'
MS   'No, you have got orange paint in your mouth. Is that a good thing to have in your mouth?'
Mel.   'Yes.' Melanie nodded. She tried to spit it on to the floor. I asked her to use a tissue, but she had managed to mix it in her mouth with large quantities of saliva and let it fall on the floor. I told her to wipe it up with a tissue, which she attempted, saying, 'Urgh!' There was still a lot in her mouth, about which she did not seem to care. She sat down saying, 'I'm ready.'
MS   'Do you want to talk about the orange paint?'
Mel.   'No, just get on with things to do.'

I had to remind her that she was not ready because she was fiddling with all sorts of things around her.

Mel. 'Do I have to fold my arms?'
MS 'Just show me you are ready.'

I asked her what she would say to someone who put orange paint in their mouth.

Mel. 'Oh, that is disgusting!' she giggled in reply, then began shrieking and banging. She was not to be drawn further and, after reminding her to sit down again, we looked at a book together. I asked Melanie who she thought the people in the picture might be.
Mel. 'Kid, dad, baby, kid, mum.'

I asked her which she would be.

Mel. 'The mum. Which would you be, Mrs Stokes?'

I told her that I am a mum so I would probably be the mum in the picture.

MS   'But you are not a mum are you?'
Mel. 'No . . . but soon I'll be a mum.'

She asked to go to the toilet. I did not respond, and she identified the people in the picture as Dora, Sam, herself (as the little girl), daddy and mum. She asked again to go to the toilet. I took her. We returned and sat at the table again and continued to look through the book until the end, and then looked at a second book, about changing a baby. Melanie said she liked this book, and said they were putting cotton wool on the baby because, 'maybe its mini is sore'. She says they were tickling the baby. When asked who she thought the people might be in the picture she started singing, 'I do not know, tra la la.'

Melanie was reluctant to continue but I commented that I thought the man in the picture was the daddy. She looked more closely and noticed the tattoos on his arms. 'Dad's got tattoos,' she added, and pointed to the tops of her arms, then to her nipples and, giggling, said, 'and one on his willy wonka, and when he pees it comes off – ha ha ha.'

She looked at the baby being powdered and said you do that to keep the baby fresh; then she started singing again, 'Keep a baby fresh . . . keep a basin flesh . . . stop.'

I said we would look at another book next week, and asked her what she would like to choose to end the session. She got out the play dough and pulled it about, trying to make 'cookies'. Suddenly she said, 'Mrs Stokes, do we have to do what teachers say?' I did not respond immediately and she went on, 'I don't want to do this any more. Can I eat it?' She pretended to eat the play dough. 'I'm not ruining it!' (cutting into the dough with scissors). She repeated that she had had enough playing with it, and I suggested that she had not given herself enough time.

Me 'I don't want to play it.'
MS 'Just sit on your chair then.'
Me 'I do want to play it.'

Melanie continued to play, asking how you make a cookie. 'I'm only asking, but I don't know how to make them,' she said in an exasperated tone. I suggested that this sounded like a rude way of talking to someone, to which she replied, 'Please may you help me make a cookie, please?'

Without waiting for a response, Melanie started shrieking, pulling out the drawers and getting up and down. We packed away the play dough and I reminded Melanie that there was only five minutes left. Melanie got out some doll's furniture and some play people. She found two small identical figures and sat them at a table, saying, 'They're going to bed in a minute.' She shouted very loudly at them, 'They've been spitting and swearing. I'm sick to death of the both of them. I'm going to bed, stupid old . . . (*indecipherable*).'

I told Melanie that our time had now ended and we would continue next time. She asked to get out another book and I repeated that we would in the next session. Together we got her coat as her escort was waiting to take her home. She lay on the floor and went limp when attempts were made to lift her. I put her hand into that of the escort. Melanie giggled and had to be almost pushed outside.

During subsequent sessions, several incidents stand out as having significance in the understanding of Melanie's state of mind. In the third session, she noticed her name on the upturned lid of her box and shrieked, 'I'm an upside-downer.' This was the first session after the half-term break and Melanie was trying to be affectionate towards me, as she spoke about cuddles being 'nice off teachers'. There were several belches during this conversation, almost to the point of vomiting. Again, Melanie had tremendous difficulty in staying on task, and was constantly trying to change the conversation. After she had done some drawing, she noticed red felt tip ink on her fingers. She spat into her hands, rubbed them together as if to clean them, then wiped them on her tee-shirt. Later, she put her fingers into her mouth, and reached to the back, where a molar was coming through. She pressed hard, and brought her fingers out with blood on them, and spat saliva and blood into her hands. I passed her a tissue, and reminded her of the incident with some orange paint in the previous session. Melanie could not respond directly to my commenting on the things she puts in her mouth, and began to squirm around on her chair and said, 'Well, I *hate* going outside (meaning our sessions). Next week you can forget me. Get somebody else.'

'I'm not going to forget you, Melanie,' I responded and repeated.

'Mrs Stokes, can I have a cuddle?' and she came sniffing to sit on my knee. 'I miss you,' Melanie added, very theatrically, in a sad and pathetic manner.

Reassurance was often sought in the sessions, and in the classroom, that we will be here tomorrow, that we won't forget her and that we look forward to seeing her. It feels as if her time in school is the only place she senses any 'containment' (Bion, 1962) or any feeling of being 'held in mind' (Winnicott, 1971).

Within the classroom, Melanie frequently spits, puts inappropriate things in her mouth, belches and makes choking noises. She often asks to go to the toilet, and I always go with her. Mostly she passes a small amount of urine, sometimes none at all. She 'acts' many dramatic parts, usually for no apparent reason, bursting into made-up songs, sobbing, screeching, shouting, yelling, swearing, frequently with hands on hips, in an adult pose, saying, 'Who do you think you are?' . . . 'What do you think you are doing?' . . . 'You can forget that!'

Our last session together was full of singing and rhythmic chanting; full of 'disgusting', 'swimming pool' and 'forgetting'. It felt very much as if she was beginning to disclose some awful things which had happened to her. She asked if she could sing into the tape recorder and then listen to it. I agreed and she began: 'Doo da doo . . . I was walking . . . what do you think you're . . . I am an old-fashioned lady . . . Sam came to the old-fashioned day . . . ' Then she began a kind of rapping chant:

'. . . and he was an old-fashioned man.
I used to spit and swear and kick but
I don't do it any more.
What is the point of doing it?
Mrs Stokes came to see . . . today . . . hee, ho, ho . . . and that is the
end of part eight.'
She started again:
'When I went to the old-fashioned shop
I met my cousin Sarah
And Joanne
I was thinking how are you.
They were in the swimming pool . . . thinking who are you?'

Melanie then asked to hear it played back. She started laughing and breathing in a rasping noise through her throat. I noticed and remarked on a bruise on her shoulder. 'Oh you shouldn't see it,' she said. When asked why, she replied, 'Because it's up to me.'

At this point, Melanie put her mouth over the corner of the tape recorder and simulated oral sex, looking at me with a conspiratorial expression.

'I keep forgetting,' she said and asked me to look at her head which she said was hurting. She immediately pulled away and said, 'Mrs Stokes you can forget it.' She began singing again, this time about spaghetti bolognese and a swimming pool. Her words, 'Oh how disgusting you are!' ended the session.

Comment

Despite the lack of actual disclosure, it is essential to remain open to the distinct possibility that Melanie has suffered sexual abuse. Her play, pictures and stories all suggest this. (Social Services have been unable to get Melanie to disclose anything to confirm their previous suspicions of sexual abuse. Consequently, no action has been taken to ensure that she is not being abused now.)

All the sessions were very difficult to control, partly at least, because of Melanie's inability to stay on task. Even choosing an activity was hard for her. Instantly her choice was made she would change her mind, and I often commented on how hard she was finding it to make choices and to maintain an interest in one activity. Many times I insisted she keep to the task. Throughout, she moved her body, stood up, fiddled with things, slid off her chair, banged her feet or her knees together, twiddled her hair, spat, shook her head and talked continuously. She frequently belched and asked for the toilet. She often burst into song for no apparent reason.

The effect of these sessions upon me was considerable. Paul Greenhalgh (1986) talks of the teacher/therapist providing a holding container for the feelings of the child. Melanie cannot describe her feelings in words, but her behaviour can tell us a tremendous amount about the state of her emotions. They are clearly unbearable and 'almost literally get pushed into the teacher'. Greenhalgh goes on to point to one of the tasks of the teacher as being: 'to demonstrate through attitude that one can have a different relationship with intolerable feelings other than being possessed by them: that they *can* be borne, tolerated and lived with, and when necessary, to hold the child when s/he got out of control until s/he could manage her/himself.'

Melanie retains unrealistic hopes of what I can provide for her. The danger of idealisation is evident in great swings of emotional states, from, 'Mrs Stokes, I love you. I wish you were my mum', to a verbal and physical attack on me when I have been absent. It is extremely difficult for her to tolerate my giving, in her perception, too much attention to another child. Towards the end of the day, when she is going to leave to go home to her family, I think she perceives this daily occurrence as me leaving her. These two dictated stories reflect a little of her feelings.

Once there was a growly lion. It was very shouty because it was not his birthday. It really wanted to be taken swimming for its birthday. Its mother could not be bothered to take it. 'I haven't got time because you get up my nose,' she said. 'So get Melanie to take you.' Melanie was in town so Mrs Stokes took her and the lion for a swim and made them happy.

Mrs Stokes was in the wood when her friend Melanie came along. Melanie walked along with Mrs Stokes and the magic woofed out of the cave. It was a snake. Then they went all the way home. They found a pool outside their garden and it growled. It was the snake. I slept at Mrs Stokes' house for 15 years.

Bowlby (1988) maintains:

> During his childhood a person learns two principal forms of behaviour and builds in his mind two principal types of model. One form of behaviour is, of course, that of a child, namely himself, interacting with a parent, his mother or his father. The corresponding working models he builds are those of himself as a child in interaction with each parent. The other form of behaviour is that of a parent, namely his mother or his father, interacting with a child, himself. The corresponding models he builds are those of each parent in interaction with himself.

Melanie's experience of such interactions must have been traumatic.

Winnicott (1971) asks: 'What does the baby see when he or she looks at the mother's face? I am suggesting that, ordinarily, what the baby sees is himself or herself. In other words the mother is looking at the baby and what she looks like is related to what she sees there. All this is too easily taken for granted.' I believe that Melanie's experience of her mother's 'mirror' was one of hatred, not of love. She was unable to provide a 'good enough' environment in which Melanie's needs could be met.

Barbara Dockar-Drysdale (1993) suggests that:

> Much violence is caused by panic states: *thinking* is an essential way of containing feelings. Communication of such thoughts to others can be an unknown safety valve – if the thoughts are not there, they cannot be communicated; the anxiety is then so terrible and primitive as to be unthinkable, and the child reaches a panic state in which he may be totally immobilised, or dreadfully active.

She goes on to suggest that the integrated child has the resources to think about and deal with feelings of panic or crisis.

The deprived, unintegrated child has no such resources. Where the integrated can *respond* to crisis, the unintegrated *reacts* to what he feels to be the threat of total annihilation. For him, conflict is not the question, but rather survival, not only of himself but of *everything*.

Perhaps Melanie is unable to think. Her unbearable thoughts cannot remain in one place long enough to do so. She does not have the resources of an integrated mind.

Melanie has presented as a very angry child for much of her life. Bowlby (1988) comments on the function of anger:

> When child or spouse behaves dangerously, an angry protest is likely to deter. When a lover's partner strays, a sharp reminder of how much he or she cares may work wonders. When a child finds himself relatively neglected in favour of the new baby, assertions of his claims may redress the balance. Thus in the right place, at the right time and in the right degree, anger is not only appropriate but may be indispensable. It serves to deter from dangerous behaviour, to drive off a rival, or to coerce a partner.

If Melanie's anger could be recognised as a protest rather than deviancy, could her needs begin to be met?

One of her most frequent expressions is, 'You can forget that!' Melanie has a lot to forget, I feel sure. Yet this is impossible for her to do. How much my brief individual interaction with her helped her to feel valued as an individual, I don't know. I have included some excerpts from our one-to-one work to illustrate some of Melanie's preoccupations that make it such a struggle for her to share me and become a member of even a small classroom group. She has begun to make relationships in a classroom where she feels safe, and seems to have managed to have internalised some feeling of being almost 'good enough' occasionally.

Chapter 9
Working with an Eight-year-old in a School Setting

ANN LEWIS

The goals [of education] are: first, to enlarge a child's knowledge, experience and imaginative understanding, and thus his awareness of moral values and capacity for enjoyment; and secondly, to enable them to enter the world as an active participant in society capable of achieving as much independence as possible. The educational needs of every child are determined in relation to these goals. The purpose of education for all children is the same; the goals are the same. But the help that individual children need in progressing towards them will be different. Whereas for some the road they travel towards the goals is smooth and easy, for others it is fraught with obstacles. For some the obstacles are so daunting that, even with the greatest help possible, they will not get very far. Nevertheless, for them too, progress will be possible, and their educational needs will be fulfilled, as they gradually overcome one obstacle after another on the way (Warnock, 1978).

The past decade and a half has seen a period of unprecedented high priority interest, concerns expressed, and legislation about education. The Government has published White Papers, Circulars, Orders and Acts, and commissioned Reports, in an attempt to overcome problems of low academic achievement, indiscipline, truancy and juvenile crime. Standards and methods of teaching have been scrutinised and criticised, curriculum content and presentation have been standardised and enforced by law. At the time of writing, under the *Education Reform Act 1988*, all schools in England and Wales are required to present a broad-based, balanced curriculum for all pupils. In theory, all children now have equal access to the education to which they are entitled within the National Curriculum, as stated in the Act. It would appear, however, that a considerable number of children are not achieving the goals set, nor are they able to make use of their access to education (Barrett, 1994). Children of all abilities are failing to learn, and are a cause of concern to parents, teachers and other professionals.

In the United Kingdom children begin school at five years of age: some are unable to cope with the transition from home to school, cannot adjust to a school system or benefit from the learning opportunities and experiences a school offers. Some make a start and then become 'stuck', others expend their energies on resisting attempts to help them learn.

As a classroom teacher in a mainstream school, numerous children puzzle and worry me. Recently, as my school's Special Needs Coordinator and therefore the 'expert' to whom my colleagues refer when they are concerned or anxious about a child's behaviour, I needed to discover the reasons behind the behaviour and its links with an inability to learn, and to define strategies which would facilitate their learning. Many such children are of average (or above) intelligence, yet they not only make little or no academic progress, but often exhibit a range of disturbing behaviours, from total withdrawal to disruptive, attention-seeking behaviour. Not only are they distressed and frustrated, but their behaviour causes distress and frustration among their teachers and their peers. In the main, these are children who do not fall into the categories and fulfil the criteria for formal assessment and a Statement of Special Educational Need and, thus, do not 'qualify' for extra help and support resources.

There is an expectation that children who fall into the SEN category will be supported within their schools with little, or no extra, resourcing. The Warnock Report on Special Educational Needs (1978) stated,

> Our conclusion that up to one child in five is likely to need special educational provision in the course of his school career does not mean that up to one in five will be handicapped in the traditional sense of the term. The majority will be unlikely to have such a long term disability or disorder. Their learning problems, which may last for varying periods of time, will stem from a variety of causes. But, unless suitable help is forthcoming, their problems will be reinforced by prolonged experience of failure (Warnock, 1978).

Currently my experience in a small rural school in the West of England suggests that the incidence is now greater than indicated by Warnock. The legislation of the National Curriculum and the formal assessment of attainments means that children who are failing to achieve what is expected of them will be more 'obvious'.

A diploma course in the use of techniques in educational therapy introduced me to an intervention which not only increased my understanding of the interactional nature of learning and teaching, but also helped me to search for links between emotional development and cognitive learning. It taught me to value and make use of some theoretical concepts. I recognised already the importance of maintaining links with other professional systems, but I believe this training has proved to be cost-effective for my school, when used for working with individuals or as a strategy within classrooms.

Central to the thinking of many educational therapists is the concept of attachment behaviour, which comes from the work of John Bowlby (1969, 1973, 1980, 1982). In this influential work on the importance of the parental relationship to mental health, Bowlby's concepts of attachment, separation and loss provide a framework for my understanding of how a child experiences early interactive learning and later learning in school.

Children referred to educational therapists usually exhibit anxious attachment behaviour (Ainsworth and Wittig, 1969) and their learning capacity, social and cognitive, is likely to be vulnerable at all stages of life. The secure child can cope with the various changes in family life, such as starting school, moving house, birth of siblings, loss of grandparents. They will exhibit appropriate levels of anxiety, but by extending and 'updating' (a concept of Bowlby's) their experience of a range of interactions they will not be overwhelmed by change.

Daniel and his Family

Daniel, to all intents and purposes, seemed to be coping in school, although his teacher noticed that he often appeared to be sad and missed school due to tummyaches, headaches or 'just feeling unwell'. He was of average intelligence, was quiet in class and accomplished just enough, except in written work, and caused minimal concern to his teacher. He presented as withdrawn, of slightly below average height, and often seemed lost in a world of his own. He had been in my class the previous year and I had also felt that he was of average ability, but felt that parental separation accounted for his quiet behaviour and reluctance to achieve. At that time I had no knowledge of his history.

Mother was invited to discuss Daniel's absences. She arrived in a state of desperation because of his behaviour at home, and his frequent reluctance to come to school. So here was an eight-year-old child who appeared to be more or less coping in school, but whose disturbed and worrying behaviour at home caused us to think again about him. Daniel has a brother, Steven, aged 18, and sisters, Laura, aged 16, and Jane, aged six.

During the interview with his mother, we discovered that Daniel's life had been beset with anxieties. At the beginning of her pregnancy, before, in fact, she realised she was pregnant, Mother underwent major surgery.

After her hospitalisation, she was on medication which caused some anxiety to the medical authorities when the pregnancy became apparent, and termination was considered. Mother was terrified of undergoing a termination, but tests then revealed that the medication had not caused any damage to the foetus, so the pregnancy continued. Immediately after mother came out of hospital, the family moved house. Mother suffered from high blood pressure and owns to having been very anxious throughout the pregnancy. Daniel's birth was normal and full term. He was breast fed for six weeks but problems of infection meant that he was subsequently bottle fed. Mother reported that he cried incessantly from about that time, and that she 'could not put him down'. She carried him around until Jane was born, when he was two-and-a-quarter years old.

Mother also reported that she and Father began to have marital problems when Daniel was about four years old and these had continued until 15 months ago, when they had separated. Daniel and his siblings all remained with mother, and the two younger children now spend time regularly with their father, staying with him, on average, one night each week. Daniel shows some ambivalence about going to stay with him. Daniel and Jane go on holiday with Father and his live-in girlfriend. The children see their father daily and he often takes them to and from school. Mother reported that Daniel is close to her and is inclined to be 'clinging'.

She considers Daniel's relationship with his siblings to be generally 'volatile'. His older sister has 'got her own problems'. When Daniel pushes her and she can't cope, she screams and shouts at him. Daniel and his younger sister have difficulty relating to each other. Mother regards herself as both mother and father to Jane, and Jane expects her full attention. Daniel's older brother has more sympathy towards, and understanding of, Daniel, and often acts as mediator in numerous family upsets.

Mother has a boyfriend, Tom, who is a widower with one daughter aged 15 and an older son who has left home. This relationship, which began a few years ago, soon after Tom's wife died, has been problematic: Mother regards Tom as very possessive, jealous and authoritarian, seeking to control those around him. 'He is inclined to bottle things up, becoming inwardly angry, until there is a verbal blow-up.' He has threatened to commit suicide if Daniel's mother leaves him. She says that Daniel is 'afraid' of him.

Daniel's behaviour at home includes verbal abuse of herself and others in the family, foul language, defecating around the house, self-injury (including tying his dressing-gown cord around his neck), and banging his head against the wall and his back against the radiators. He was cruel to the family's pet hamster – tying it to a 'parachute' and throwing it up in the air, putting it under water and holding it by one leg.

She frequently had difficulty getting him to school and was worried because she couldn't tell if he was genuinely unwell or using it as an excuse to stay at home.

In my assessment of Daniel's learning skills, I discovered that he had a reading and vocabulary age of 8 years, and a spelling age of 7 years. He achieved a maximum score in copying and recognising geometric shapes. In another test in the Aston Index (Revised) (Newton and Thomson, 1982) Goodenough Draw-a-Man test, Daniel drew a picture of a man at a level one might expect from a six-year-old. It is interesting to note, however, that a week later, when I asked him to draw a picture of his family, he drew them all in profile. This portrayal of people indicated a more mature level of drawing. There seemed to be a clear discrepancy between the two.

My next task was to think about my own experience of him in my class. I felt Daniel had probably formed an anxious attachment to his mother and was still unable to cope with the loss of his father. Was this affecting his capacity to make full use of the learning opportunities and experiences which were provided for him in school, or were there other factors?.

Thinking about Daniel

In order to take on the role of 'educational attachment figure' for Daniel, and to provide a 'second-chance learning' experience, concepts from the work of Barrett and Trevitt (1991), it was necessary to consider the structure of the sessions and the provision of appropriate materials and activities for use within them. The importance of the boundaries of time, place and privacy were explained to the whole school staff, and arrangements made for a room to be available at the same time each week. The next part of the preparation was suggested during the group supervision we received in the latter part of our diploma training. I provided Daniel with a box for his exclusive use which contained animal families and fencing (some use doll families), felt pens, pencils, blunt-ended scissors, Sellotape, eraser, elastic bands, paper clips, glue, Plasticine, a pack of playing cards and a pencil sharpener. Specially selected books and some plain paper were always available.

This box has a lid which can be labelled as the child wishes and can become an important part of the therapeutic process. Daniel labelled his, 'Daniel's Box. Private. Keep Out.' For most children it becomes a symbolic container of their feelings as well as a place to store things they have made during sessions, often a tangible confirmation of their achievements.

We were to work in the 'special needs' room, (used to facilitate work with small groups or individual children, by school staff or external professionals such as Educational Psychologists, Special Needs Advisory

Teachers, Audiologists). It is situated between two departments of the school and is sometimes used as a passageway between them.

The first session

I collected Daniel from his classroom for our first session, explained what we would be doing during our special time together and that we would meet at the same time and place for an hour each week. I showed him his box and explained that it was for his exclusive use, and also showed him the other materials which were available. I said we would begin each week with some reading, writing and spelling activities: he would then be able to choose what he wanted to do. I also said that I would tell him when we reached five minutes before the end of each session.

We discussed his difficulty in writing things down, and I suggested that he might 'tell' a story, which I would write for him, and print on the computer before the next session. We could then make a book of his stories over the coming weeks. My aim during this introductory session was to begin to establish a base, and to create a 'working space' in which we could rediscover his lost learning skills, a 'shared space where we could interact, where feelings could be expressed and tasks completed' (Barrett and Trevitt 1991).

During our first few sessions together, I became very aware of the phenomena of transference and counter-transference (Freud, 1926). Towards the end of the second session I was aware that I had been left with feelings of almost overwhelming sadness and despair. I learned during my training in educational therapy techniques that feelings from early childhood are usually transferred on to others during our interactions with one another, and that these feelings, both good and bad, can affect our ability to function satisfactorily. I understood that similar feelings can be elicited in the counter-transference, which helped me to tolerate what I was experiencing in my work with Daniel. I understood also that I could make use of these concepts for my own learning.

During the first two sessions there was very little verbal interaction between us, and Daniel only spoke in response to remarks from me. When dictating his stories there were long silences, and during the first session I prompted him by wondering what would happen next, or what the characters might be feeling. In the second session I found the silences quite painful, but decided, nevertheless, to prompt him less in his story-writing time and during his choosing time; I considered that I should respect his silence and his space, in order not to intrude upon his thoughts. Throughout the time I have been working and interacting with Daniel, I have particularly considered the process of his communication with me. It began with little or no communication, a period of silence, stemming from mistrust and/or anxiety, then the non-verbal behaviour of smiling started, along with communication through play and use of the metaphor in his stories. Verbal interaction began by talking metaphorically about his fears, until he began speaking of his actual fears and frightening experiences.

Our first two sessions together showed the communication through silence, and although he smiled occasionally during these, it was not until the end of the fourth session, which took place after a two-week break, that he smiled with his eyes as well as his mouth. This session had begun with me collecting him, as usual, from his classroom, and I had arrived just as he was being publicly reprimanded by his class teacher. The first part of the session had been tense and somewhat strained, and even in the latter part I had felt we had taken a step backward. While he played with the Lego, he sat on the floor with his legs curled under him and a tense look on his face. He made no attempt to communicate with me, either verbally, or by eye contact, unless I spoke to him. I wondered aloud if he was finding it difficult to be back in school after his holiday. He looked at me, shrugged his shoulders, and turned away. Later I remarked, half to myself, that he seemed rather quiet and sad today. He replied, 'No', without looking at me. At the end of the session he tidied up very slowly and carefully, replaced his Lego model in his box, and returned the Lego box to its place on the shelf. I said I would see him next week at the same time, and as he went to the door, he hesitated, looked back, and smiled for the first time with his eyes, said 'See ya' and left. I felt that in spite of the difficulties for both of us in dealing with our feelings in this session, he showed at the end that he felt secure enough to show another side of himself, and that our communication was progressing. I also felt that the closing sentence in his story could possibly be a symbolic reference to the security of the sessions. (During group supervision I recognised that I should have taken up Daniel's feelings about his public reprimand and the two-week break.) During the next two sessions he chose Play People in his 'choosing' time, and enacted a series of motor accidents, pedestrians being knocked over, and car and motorbike accidents, alongside a group of children on swings and roundabouts in a playground. On one occasion, he placed a group of children side by side at the beginning of his race track and I wondered who was looking after them. He replied, 'They're on their own.' A little later he added, 'But one of the mummies in the playground will keep an eye on them.'

Throughout these sessions with the Play People he returned, repeatedly, to set the roundabout in motion. I felt that he was symbolically showing me his fear of being deserted or of losing his mother, but wondered whether he too felt like the perpetually revolving roundabout – getting nowhere. I felt we had progressed to communication through play. His stories in the first eight sessions were about animals who were lost while out playing, or were swooped on by predators; about people who got lost or in difficulties and had to be rescued; about writing stories and drawing pictures, and about being frightened of the dark.

In session nine, he wrote a story about a baby dragon.

> The little red dragon crawled slowly from its egg, crawled slowly out of its nest and looked around. It looked around and saw a big dragon. It was its mother. Its mother picked it up and put it on her back and flew out of the cave. It was amazed when it looked down at the countryside below and a little bit frightened. Soon it was time for them to go back to the nest because it was getting dark. When they got back to the nest they rested for a month's sleep.

I wondered if, metaphorically, I was the mother dragon, and Daniel the baby dragon emerging in a different way. The different stages of the progression of our communication inevitably overlapped. Later he drew two very interesting pictures both of which consisted mainly of a vast amount of sky coloured red, orange, yellow, blue and green, with small silhouettes in the foreground, one of a person standing on a rock, the other of a rock formation. Throughout this activity he talked continuously.

Two weeks before the Christmas break, Daniel communicated his fears of frightening experiences for the first time, when he told me he remembered when he was a little baby and had to go to hospital and had tubes in him. He also told me how worried he had been when his mother was hospitalised on two occasions. In the following session he talked and asked questions about angels, evil spirits, poltergeists, ouija boards, and drugs, and spoke of being frightened of being in bed in the dark, 'In case an evil spirit came.'

Now we had reached communication outside the metaphor I felt somewhat disturbed by the fears being expressed. (I knew that Daniel's paternal grandfather had been mentally unstable.) Had I been working in a multi-disciplinary team I could have conferred with colleagues about my own fears. The only recourse open to me as a teacher in a school was to enlist the understanding of the head teacher for the referral of Daniel to an outside agency.

While working with Daniel I learned the value of allowing a child his silent space. I felt Daniel, too, recognised that the silence became facilitating. Being able to hold him and his fears in mind between sessions was an important facet of my learning. Again, Daniel seemed to learn that he, too, could hold another person in mind when faced with separation at the end of each session, as well as through longer breaks. By reflecting and mirroring our shared experiences and interactions, he has been able to discover that it is safe for him to own them. This concept of 'holding in mind' is taken from Winnicott (1965).

Conferring with Daniel's class teacher (without breaking the confidentiality of Daniel's sessions), led to a realisation by her, of how troubled he was by fears unrelated to classroom tasks. Once it became apparent that we could rediscover Daniel's 'lost' learning skills; he began to read with enthusiasm, wrote voluntarily, and his behaviour in school became less withdrawn. His mother reported 'improvements' in his behaviour at home. Even this relatively short intervention, using educational therapy techniques, will help Daniel, I feel, to become more emotionally secure and thus enable him to develop his learning skills and overcome his difficulties.

Involving other staff and other professionals

In many ways, Daniel does not appear to be typical of most children who are, or may be, referred for educational therapy. He was not causing a great deal of concern in school, either academically or by his behaviour; he had not been the subject of staffroom discussion, nor had he been referred for informal or formal assessment; he was neither disruptive nor totally withdrawn, neither was there any involvement with Social Services or Health Services.

In explaining some of the techniques that I would be using I found that many of my colleagues, though sympathetic to my new understanding of the possible links between attachment behaviour and the interactional learning process, had some difficulty in accepting, or understanding, the concept or the process.

Although the importance of the boundaries of time, place and privacy were explained to all the staff before Daniel and I began our sessions together, there were several occasions when our space was intruded upon, timetables altered so we could not meet at the regular time, or our room was required by someone else. However I valued having opportunities to monitor and evaluate the effectiveness of the intervention with Daniel's class teacher, who, I felt, reconsidered the possible links between children's experiences and their learning.

Comments

There have been important lessons learned from this first experience of using educational therapy techniques as an intervention within the school. My diploma training will enable me to act as facilitator within the whole staff group. We can make links for SEN children with an emotional, as well as an educational understanding. Another possibility is the setting up of an informal parent support group. An increasing number of parents are appealing to their children's teachers for advice and help in coping with their children at home, in addition to being distressed by their behaviour in school. A parent support group, meeting regularly, would offer parents the opportunity to exchange their experiences with one another and to talk to members of staff informally in a non-threatening situation. The setting up of an 'open clinic' in school, where teachers bring to the whole staff group any areas of concern, if run in parallel, could prove invaluable if a child or parents' difficulties became more serious. By a process of joint exploration, members of staff would be able to answer for themselves the questions raised, rather than automatically having others answering for them. They would thus be enabled to see how they might make better use of their own skills and the therapeutic side of educational methods and relationships (Hanko, 1990).

Ideally other professionals, such as health visitors, general practitioners, social workers, educational psychologists, school doctors and nurses, and others, could be involved in discussions as an early preventative measure for distressed families. If a mutual trust can be engendered between school staff and parents, they too would acquire a greater understanding of the work of other professionals.

I feel it is important that when teachers make use of an educationally therapeutic intervention, there should be a support system available for discussion with those who understand the psychodynamic approach and process, (unless such teachers can be offered a clinical training). It is easy to become overwhelmed by the feelings engendered during the interactive process of individual work. (There is no clinical training available in the South West.)

The Effectiveness of Educational Therapy Training

My class has 32 7- to 8-year-olds, some of whom behave inappropriately or cannot achieve what is expected of them. As a Special Needs Coordinator, I have often been at a loss when asked for help with disruptive or withdrawn behaviour, or children who cannot even attempt to complete a task. I was unable to see beyond the way in which they presented themselves. Even when I have been aware of some children's home difficulties or other problems, like many other teachers, I have been guilty of saying, 'We can't do anything to change things because of their family background.' I have felt myself becoming irritated or angry for no apparent reason when dealing with some children. I have become impatient with attention-seeking behaviour and over-protective with immature and tearful children. My interactions with some children have been more negative than positive.

The *Elton Report on Discipline in Schools* (1989) highlighted the need for in-service training courses for teachers, to extend and promote their understanding of children's emotional and behavioural difficulties, and to give training in techniques of pupil management, in order to reduce both teacher and pupil stress. There has been much publicity recently about the increase in truancy and violence among children, suggesting that schools are failing to motivate their pupils.

Since my diploma training I have learned to try and understand why children behave in a certain way, wonder what they are feeling during that behaviour, and question my own reactions to it. I would like the thinking, theory and practice of educational therapy to become a component of initial teacher training. Newly qualified teachers should enter the classroom prepared by their training to cope with children's emotional and behavioural difficulties, and to understand the effect that loss, family discord and socio-economic factors can have on cognitive skills. They should understand, too, how feelings elicited can change their responses during interactions. This could be a major contribution to their behaviour and to the development of their teaching skills, and enable children to achieve the goals of education, as defined in the Warnock Report (1978) with which I began this chapter.

Since undertaking training in educational therapy, I have learned to ask why a child behaves in a certain way, to wonder what they are feeling when they behave as they do, to look at my own reactions to different behaviour, and thus to interact more appropriately. My own learning about such concepts as anxious attachment behaviour, holding, working space, transference and counter-transference, has led me to look at and understand the behaviour of children in the classroom, and my own, in a different way. In taking on board the idea that children's emotional development is linked to cognitive learning and the acquisition of social skills, I no longer jump to conclusions or react without thinking. My work with Daniel enabled me to recognise that my class contains many other Daniels. I have been able to ask questions to which, it would appear, there are answers.

When a classroom becomes an educational 'secure base' (Bowlby, 1988) with teachers as 'educational attachment figures' (Barrett and Trevitt, 1991) for all children in a class, the majority can learn cognitively and explore creatively, the few may be able to rediscover their learning capacity.

At a time when it would appear that the number of children with learning problems caused by emotional and behavioural difficulties is increasing, and schools have a greater responsibility in providing support for these children, I believe that training in educational therapy would be an invaluable resource in any school. As was stated earlier in this study, the *Warnock Report on Special Educational Needs* (1978) stated the importance of early intervention in children's learning problems. The use of educational therapy techniques could prevent short-term problems becoming long-term, major difficulties.

In the case of Daniel, the problem behaviours he presented at home were far more worrying than his behaviour and academic reluctance in school. It was, however, because of his mother's concern becoming so great that she brought it into school, that we were able to recognise that what we were seeing in school was indeed an early warning signal that he had a problem, and we were able to provide the necessary intervention. Had it not been for my educational therapy training, we may well have missed the opportunity to provide the early intervention which Daniel needed.

The child whose behaviour is disruptive and attention-seeking in the classroom can hardly be ignored. Often he is dealt with in punitive and rejecting ways without any thought being given to the reasons for his behaviour. In educational therapy, thought is given to the concept of systems. In any family system there is a process of hierarchy, a set of rules, an ethos, a set of boundaries. A child learns to fit within the family system and behaves accordingly; his behaviour is not an isolated thing, it is controlled by the context in which it occurs. Each part of the system the child is in is affected by, and affects, the child and his behaviour. When a child first enters school, he enters a new system with a new hierarchy, new rules, new boundaries and a new ethos. These may be very different from those of the family system, and for an anxiously attached child the changes may be impossible to manage. Behaviour management may work for some children, for example those with poor parenting or poor social skills, but for a child with emotional problems they are inappropriate because he is unequipped to respond to them. By using educational therapy as an intervention for the child with disruptive behaviour and learning problems, the child is enabled to modify his behaviour as well as recover his learning skills, learning to tolerate and manage change through the interactive teacher/child dyad.

The withdrawn child is much more likely to be overlooked, as may well have happened in Daniel's case. In fact the withdrawn child usually works at being ignored. The withdrawn behaviour may be the result of earlier experiences of rejection, ignoring or smothering by the child's attachment figure. He may have feelings of anger, guilt, despair, fear or chaos. In most cases, because they cause no trouble in class, these children are able to withdraw into anonymity. With more emphasis being placed on children's ability to cooperate and work with others, to ask questions and to discuss what they are doing or have done, within the National Curriculum assessment process, there is a more desperate need than ever to be able to offer help and support to these learning-disabled children. Again, I believe that the use of educational therapy techniques would prove an invaluable intervention for these 'forgotten' children in our classrooms.

Educational therapy can, in my opinion, be a most effective intervention, and, from my own experience, can rescue, from a 'no hope' situation, children whose needs would often not be considered serious enough for formal assessment and a Statement of Educational Need. Training in educational therapy techniques provides teachers with a means of dealing with the very problems which in the past have caused them distress, anxiety and frustration, enabling them to interact more positively and appropriately with all the children in their care. It can also often be of benefit in teachers' relationships with parents and with other professionals. By learning about the interactive nature of learning and teaching, about the links between emotional development and cognitive learning, about attachment behaviour, transference and counter-transference, about the importance of boundaries, about holding, reflecting and mirroring, about the interaction of systems and about the importance of managing change, I believe that I have been more effectively prepared to cater for the diverse needs of Special Needs pupils, to provide better-quality teaching and pastoral care for my class, and to understand my own feelings in interactive situations. I believe that my relationships with my colleagues, with other professionals, and with parents, have effectively been enhanced, and that my training in educational therapy has opened new doors within my own school for a different approach in seeking to help learning-disabled children.

Conclusion

The *Elton Report on Discipline in Schools* (1989) highlighted the need for in-service training courses for teachers, to extend and promote their understanding of children's emotional and behavioural difficulties, and to give training in techniques of pupil management in order to reduce both teacher and pupil's stress. There has been much publicity in recent months about the increase in violence among children, the number of children failing in school, and disciplinary problems. It is my opinion that training in educational therapy techniques should be an important part of initial teacher training. If newly qualified teachers come into the classroom prepared by their training to cope with the problems which may arise because of children's emotional and behavioural difficulties, prepared to look beyond the inappropriate behaviours or learning disabilities of some children to the possible causes for them, then the children of the future have a greater chance of achieving the goals of education as defined in the Warnock Report of 1978 and in fulfilling their educational potential, thus enabling them to take their rightful places as full members of society.

Chapter 10
Bringing Educational Therapy into the Classroom

LINDA LAW

Working with a Bereaved Six-year-old Boy

When someone dies their family is thrown into great confusion. They find themselves embarking on the stages of grief by expressing anger, protest, despair or denial, and attempting to search for the lost member until they can move towards an acceptance of the loss and to a subsequent recovery. When a young child dies, tremendous pain and guilt overlay all these stages. Kübler-Ross (1983) gives a hypothetical account of the confusion that descends to 'protect' the parents from having to think about the loss. 'After the death of a child, the world seems to stand still and if anything moves around us it is not meant for us. We mechanically walk the dog, put a coat on our first-grader and send him off to school; we absent mindedly put the coffee on and "answer the phone in a daze".' Likewise, Rando (1985) suggests some reasons for the suffering of parents. 'When a young child dies, the unique dynamics of the parent–child relationship cause parents to feel they have lost not only a child but also a part of themselves. Because parents believe their children to be an extension of themselves, the loss inflicts a devastating narcissistic injury – the child has died "out of turn".'

It is easy to see why the mind prefers to be 'absent' when the thinking through of the issue is so painful. With a child's death comes the cessation of the need to function as that child's parent, and the very identity of the parent may then be threatened. Bernstein et al. (1989) state: 'More painful still, the loss threatened their sense of being an adequate parent, having been unable to fulfil parental duties of protection and nurturance'. They go further: 'As a result, many parents experience tremendous guilt that may be completely unrelated to any objective responsibility for the child's death.'

The energy involved in dealing, or preventing oneself from having to deal, with such feelings, and the overwhelming exhaustion and dazedness that abound can leave parents emotionally unavailable to surviving siblings, even though they may be outwardly available, performing such tasks as described by Kübler-Ross (1983) in a perfunctory manner. I think the experience of Nathan, who I shall write about later in this chapter, is summed up by Pollock's (1986) survey:

> In childhood sibling loss, the effects of the loss are mediated through different members of the family . . . in addition (to the loss) the surviving sibling is often faced with the task of coping with the loss of parents who, because of their intense grief, may be unable to meet the surviving sibling's needs. Possibly the greatest fear is brought home to the child by the words of Rosen (1986): 'The unavailability of the parents may cause a child to feel that his or her existence is in question.'

Spinetta and Spinetta (1981) point out that if a child's death is preceded by a time of long illness the siblings can face parental unavailability some time before the death occurs:

> Siblings of children with a life-threatening illness often face the developmental tasks necessary to achieve adulthood alone. Their attempts to seek help are often met with a plea to be mature and generous, and to respect the needs of the dying child. Even the mentally strong and healthy child cannot be expected to go through life's transitional stages without support from parents.

This thinking is extended by Bernstein et al. (1989), who noted that well siblings experience the attention given to a dying child as a rejection of themselves, . . . 'and are left alone to deal with the thought that they too will become seriously ill and die'.

Nathan and his Family

Nathan lived with his parents and one sister. His other sister, Sarah, died, when two years old, a few months after Nathan's birth. Rachel was born three years later. His parents are a professional couple, attractive in appearance, who felt that their son's learning difficulties, tantrums and hysterical defiance sprang from an 'emotional source'. They were resistant to family therapy and felt Nathan made things difficult for himself. Father was experienced at protecting his wife and would only accept help if the focus remained on Nathan, saying, 'We've no time for all this fuss', an attitude confirmed by Bernstein et al: 'The extraordinary pain involved in examining what goes on in the family, and uncovering the buried grief, can cause parents to avoid coming for treatment, or to end it prematurely. Failure to address the death often results in the lingering-presence of a ghost, working its mischief in many ways.' They say also, 'The goal for grieving families is to help them turn the ghost of the lost child into a memory, freeing the energies of parents and siblings for loving relationships, further development and creative living' (Bernstein et al., 1989). It seemed that they had been unable to spend time with their children because of their work commitments. (If any of the children were ill and unable to attend the nursery school, their grandmother travelled several hundred miles to come and look after them.) Mother said, 'Nathan had been an intense, demanding baby, refusing to feed from the breast and cried day and night for months.' At the time of our meeting mother still found him an 'irritating and uncooperative little boy'. Nathan identified very strongly with his mother, and could not accept that he was not in charge of her. Nathan's parents were unwilling to continue family discussions. I thought that educational therapy might help Nathan to begin this 'freeing' process as a bereaved school child.

Nathan in a School Special Unit

Nathan was placed in a special unit when he was five years of age (he transferred to a mainstream school at seven). He presented himself in an assessment session as a quiet, eager boy of average build, with fair hair, small features and pale eyes. Each school day was a struggle to seize power from any adult, a screaming objection to any suggestion of schoolwork, and a generally fearful and angry avoidance of his classmates. This behaviour became difficult to resolve; if the upset occurred in the morning the end of the day would still see Nathan scarlet and glaring, stiff with rage, or sullenly silent. Mother expressed a wish not to be contacted as she felt tantrums would mean she would have to come and take Nathan home.

We discovered that this little boy knew that his mother's first baby was a girl and that she was dead. He did not appear to have a real understanding of death. He claimed, on one occasion, that his mother had killed the baby by letting it get too cold, and on another by making it eat real food when it should have had milk. He also said the baby spoke to him when the family went to the grave. He thought the baby lived in heaven, but also insisted that there was no such place. After almost two years at the special unit, Nathan was at appropriate levels for his age in most subjects except reading, in which he was still at a very basic level, able to recognise sounds, but not to blend them or use them to decode words. His favourite subject was maths, with the exception of the concepts relating to time. He enjoyed handling money although he avoided estimating or predicting. When asked to do this, and finding the results inaccurate, he altered the estimation to coincide with the actuality.

To assist Nathan's transfer to mainstream school, his parents agreed to my seeing him for seven, one-hour sessions of an educational therapy nature. (This was to be a component of my diploma training in educational therapy techniques, for which I received group supervision, to which I shall refer from time to time.) Prior to this offer, my course tutor helped me to consider the problems that may be encountered when a child is working in therapeutic sessions with his teacher's classroom assistant. It was hoped that these would be balanced by the advantage of my being able to see the effect on the child's play and learning in class.

Nathan did, in fact, have difficulty separating the sessions from daily class routines. He tended to bring the 'metaphorical environment' from the educational therapy approach to any one-to-one reading with me. The class teacher with whom I worked, and I, were pleased that the rest of the class not only tolerated Nathan's monopoly of one of us very well, but seemed to gain hope that they too could one day progress through their difficulties.

The first session

I had explained why we were having this special time together, and how I hoped we could use it. (We worked in a corner of the cloakroom set up with a very small table and two chairs; Nathan chose to sit with his back to the stairs.) He looked eagerly at the books I had provided but only glanced at the box with the usual contents.

L.L.   'Who do you think is best at reading in your class?'
N.   'You.'
L.L.   'Out of the children?'
N.   'Well I'd like to say its me, but I suppose I can't.'
L. L.   'Who is best then?'
N.   'Alan.' (Alan is a complete non-reader and hardly speaks at all.)
N.   'I'm the best at maths, though, because I go to college, a little college, every night and practise. I do a lot.'

Later in this session Nathan was invited to choose a story to be read to him. He chose *Postman Pat*, and squealed in a baby voice excitedly, 'Wead dis one to Nafun'. The story was long, repetitive, with a series of events, and a predictable ending. Part way through Nathan interrupted, 'Excuse me, Mrs Law. I don't understand any of that at all. What's it about? I don't know it'.

I gave a précis but Nathan claimed he could not understand it. We acted the events and he said, 'Now I know it, but not in the book.' In the group discussion (supervision) it was suggested that Nathan saw himself as my 'equal', by acknowledging me as the best reader and placing me among the children. I felt he had shown me contempt by placing me with a non-reader. Perhaps he also identified with me as he knew I, with some colleagues, was attending college.

Classroom reading with Nathan

Following this session in his class reading lesson, he cheerily progressed through the books without any comment other than to read the text. He read *Little Red Hen* in the Ladybird *Read it Yourself* series. He began by 'sounding out' the letters and managed the rest from pictorial clues. He found the story utterly absorbing as it concerns a trick on the hen, and then her revenge, by trickery, on the fox. Nathan tended to regard all work as laden with tricks and traps: 'Ah! They're trying to catch me out,' or, 'They want me to say this, but it's a trick', being frequent remarks, even for the most innocuous books and worksheets. Bettelheim states: 'What the teacher views as the child's inability . . . the child views as a trap, deliberately set to catch him making an error' (Bettelheim and Zelan, 1982).

The second session

I asked Nathan to look at graded picture books with short phrases accompanying each page. As the most frequent image was of a mother at home, playing with, or cooking for, a baby, it was hoped that he would respond to these pages and that these issues could be thought about together. He made no response until he read a book about men and women at work. The picture of a child dressing up in front of a mirror led to the following exchange:

N. 'What can she do? She could light a fire if she wanted, and burn the house down . . . except she's not at home, you can see she's got her school clothes on underneath, look!'

L.L. 'Do you think she could light a fire if she was at home?'
N. 'She might . . .she could if she wanted to.'
L.L. 'Would you light a fire at home?'
N. 'She could or she could do cooking.' (He then reads on quickly.)

The second picture depicted a fireman with a hosepipe standing in a pool of water.

N. 'A fireman. He lights fires.'
L.L. 'You think he lights fires?'
N. 'Oh no! He puts them out. Fires burn all the houses down. Dear, dear. Funny really.'

The next picture shows a woman dragging a baby-buggy through deep snow. The caption reads, 'What does she do with the baby?'

N.   'Oh, look! Heavy snow . . . she's gone out in heavy snow.'

L.L.   'Why do you think she'd go out with a baby in heavy snow? It's a real snowstorm isn't it?'

N.   'It must be an emergency . . . a fire. There's a fire, and she has to take the baby with her in the snow.'

L.L.   'Is their house on fire?'

N.   'No. They know where there's a fire and they're going to it.'

L.L.   'Why are they going?'

N.   'Because they love fires. They just love fires. Do you?'

L.L.   'I wouldn't like my house to be on fire.'

N.   'Oh, they do. They like it best.'

The rest of the session was taken up with a matching game and I read *Cinderella* to Nathan. He had earlier referred to ashes and I connected this to the story but he denied all knowledge of the story. He commented that the ugly sisters would do anything 'to spoil her (Cinderella's) life'.

In the classroom

At the end of that day he asked to take the book home because his mummy didn't know the story. He returned it the next morning, saying his father had read it to him, but that his mother read it to herself. He said 'She got it mixed up with *Sleeping Beauty*. She said you'd tell me that one because she's got to go out and I don't know it.' The story was read to him.

Nathan often dressed up in a flouncy dress. He did this again and, as usual, this was followed by a visit to the toilet in the main school. On his return he made several play-telephone calls, making demands such as, 'Well, get it right now or I'll never speak to you again', or (to classmate Alan), 'Go to work husband, for goodness sake. Dearie, Dearie, get out to work.' Anything more hateful in the way 'Dearie' was spoken it is hard to imagine! On this occasion Alan was given a doll to look after in the role of Dearie. Nathan returned from 'shopping'. He enjoyed handling coins, 'buying' groceries and then burying the doll in the pram underneath the load.

N. 'Here, you have this. I don't like children,' as he handed Alan the doll.

A.   'It's dead.'

N.   'So what?'

A.   'What shall we do?'

N.   'Oh, for goodness sake, just bury it and make something up!'

In the next session, acting on the group supervision suggestion to try some work on opposites, it was possible to think with Nathan about fire and its 'scariness' and to wonder about feeling scared when pretending begins to get real. Wondering about how people would like us if they knew what we were like inside produced a sudden outburst, 'I never said "Fire!" I wouldn't say it. I'm not allowed to and I don't know it!'

He was unable to get to grips with a model train he had started, and loved making, so was offered a story. He chose *Heidi*, 'Because of the little girl on the cover,' asking, 'Is this boring?' Having been told that some parts were exciting, while he might find others less so, he settled down to listen and became enthralled, shouting 'No!' when Aunt Deta comes to reclaim Heidi. He grabbed the book and searched the page to see what happened next. 'Oh please, please don't say she's going! Does it say she's got to?'

When Heidi becomes homesick and walks in her sleep, the doctor tells her, 'You are very sick, little girl, are you unhappy?' She replies, 'I'm not allowed to say that.'

Nathan nodded vigorously, whispering, 'Poor Heidi. It's awful, I know.' Peter's attempt to keep the handicapped, older Clara away from him and Heidi met with approval from Nathan although he looked shocked. He was surprised when everyone forgave Peter, saying, 'It was only jealousy and he had got over it now.'

At the end of the story Nathan asked if he could read. Then he said, 'I hate going to bed. It's not fair.' He went on to say that there was no bedtime story, but his little sister pestered him to read to her. He said she did this to tease him as she is the better reader. Then he sighed and asked, 'You can read all the books in the world, can't you?' adding, 'Mummy can't read very well.'

L.L.   'Why do you think that?'
N.   'Well, she gets difficult, she, you know, when there's a word, she . . . it's difficult. She gets, she just, she gets . . . '
L.L.   'Stuck?'
N.   'Yes, and she just stops.'

And so did he. He worked on the model train and did not speak again. He remained silent back in the classroom, even at home time.

After presenting this session to my members' training group, it seemed that Nathan had been very frightened at one point; so much so that he could not begin a much-enjoyed activity, because he was being asked too much, too quickly. Having compared my omnipotence with his mother's, and (in his view) her poor reading, possibly the guilt he felt at being 'disloyal' left him beset with the problem he attributed to his mother – not knowing what to say next. (It was pointed out to us that the transference of these feelings may have been what had made me supply the end to his sentence, having found myself uneasy and anxious when watching his struggle.) As the sessions continued, Nathan began to read fairly fluently, asking to be tested and requesting flashcards. He maintained a 'wanting to control' attitude but was willing to put this aside after the first few minutes. He worked on making his wooden train and this seemed to give him terrific satisfaction. He had begun to write, albeit almost entirely phonetically, and could complete this work without the tears and the sullenness it had previously engendered.

In the next session Nathan came in saying, happily, that Mummy had bought him a video of *Cinderella* and a cassette tape about *Beauty* – Did I know the story?

L.L.	'Has it got a monster in it?'
N.	'No! It's lovely.'
L.L.	'Is there a princess?'
N.	'No, it's about a horse.'
L.L.	'Oh, Black Beauty. Is it sad?'
N.	'No. It's lovely, and it's very short.'
L.L.	'The Black Beauty I know is sad and very long; perhaps it's not the same on your tape.'
N.	'Tell it to me. I love stories. It's very good.'
L.L.	'How's the train going along? We can finish some of the painting today if we get going. I'll get some paints.'

I left Nathan, briefly, to fetch the paints and found myself several times going to get other things from the adjacent room. In an effort to counter the boredom I felt during this session I invited Nathan to dictate a story about a train, which I would write down. He responded enthusiastically to this suggestion, saying, after a moment, 'Once upon a time there was a train, and it went to the seaside and it had a cup of tea and it went home and had spaghetti bolognese.' When he saw that this was faithfully written he said, 'Oh! Don't put that. It's silly. I meant it to be stupid.' He could not think of anything to add so stood back to admire the train, saying, 'Isn't she a Byoody?'

When I responded, 'She certainly is a beauty' Nathan cried 'Oh! Beauty is . . . is . . . it's the same! Let's call her *Colourful Beauty*!' This was written for him on cards, which were attached to each side of the train, and then coloured by Nathan with great care, and became the title of the story. He then said he was ready to do the story, but the bell rang to signal 'home time'. He was annoyed at this because he had not been given a five-minute warning and now had to go 'when it's all getting good'.

With the supervision group I said I knew that this session was badly handled by the counter-transference brought to it. Several members of the group pointed out that *Black Beauty* may have been a very meaningful story for Nathan – beginning with the loss of a special older sibling, the idyllic bliss of early childhood, and the near death of Beauty through neglect. The various trials of despair and poverty, loneliness and confusion, that Beauty underwent and overcame, and the observations on the death of Ginger, may also have helped Nathan. It does seem a tailor-made story for a boy in his situation, with a male as the main character, but my perception of the story led to my being unable to see this potential. When Nathan had first mentioned the tape I had assumed it might be *Black Beauty* but hoped it wasn't. I remembered the story as being full of gratuitous misery, mawkish, and deliberately tear-jerking. Having read Anna Sewell's biography by Chitty (1971), I was struck by the bitterness, anger and self-pity of Sewell. I felt it had infected the text of the story, and just thinking of it made me uneasy.

In the light of the comments from the group, I was helped to understand that I was trying to outdo the parents by being able to read to him, often, spend time alone with him, and being a 'better' parent by choosing suitable books. Whatever it was that *Black Beauty* had occasioned, I had not been able to 'hold' the session and found myself wishing I were not present. Nathan's willingness to be left, and my 'unavailability' masked his resentment as seen in his 'stupid' story, perhaps feeling, 'I can't be bothered with you if you can't be bothered with me.' Difficulties not belonging to, or brought by, the child had muddled the adult's thinking, causing the haphazard nature of the session and its subsequent overrunning. In spite of my 'failure' as the adult, Nathan had behaved excellently, managing to stay 'held' and almost succeeding in reaching a very positive resolution to the session. The next session began with an apology by me, to Nathan, an assurance that there would be no to-ing and fro-ing, and an admiration for his resourceful and good attitude. He generously accepted the apology with none of his previous high-handedness.

Bettelheim and Zelan (1982) maintain that children can make use of almost any working dyad when a verbal link allows them to own their feelings. It is this verbal link that seems to provide the means of looking beyond the script in the story, bringing out into a thinking space some preoccupation that the child alone cannot think about. How much the verbal link was re-enforced, because I worked also with Nathan in the classroom, is impossible to assess.

In our sessions Nathan found three stories particularly helpful: *The Pied Piper, Heidi* and *Rapunzel*, and a lot of work was done around these. After a discussion about 'value', Nathan's misreading of 'mummy' for 'money', and vice versa, stopped. He questioned the actions of Rapunzel's parents and, perhaps through them, his own. Of importance to him was the happiness of the children 'stolen' by the Pied Piper, and how much the lame child envied them. In *Heidi* the servant's mistaking the sleepwalking girl for a little ghost led to a series of questions and thoughts about the existence of ghosts, where people were after they died, and how remembering things, and people, could be managed. 'Failure to address the death often results in the lingering presence of a ghost, working its mischief in many ways' (Bernstein et al., 1989). Referring to psychotherapy with the bereaved, these authors continue,

'The goal for grieving families is to help them turn the ghost of the lost child into a memory, freeing the energies of parents and siblings for loving relationships, further development and creative living.'

In each session Nathan worked on *Colourful Beauty*. At times he would insist that the colours be chosen for him, and in one session he painted on my arm, speaking in his 'Dearie' voice, 'What a mess you've got yourself into! What will your mother say?' I replied that since my mother lived 300 miles away she would not be in a position to say very much but I thought I would leave the paint on my arm and wash it off some other time. When Nathan enquired what mother would say if anyone asked about it I replied, 'Oh, this is some paint like *Colourful Beauty* has.' Nathan dabbed some on his hand and said, 'I'll say that too. We can both think of her. We can be proud of her, can't we?'

This train, very significantly, lacked wheels, despite many fine items having been collected for the purpose. In the sessions working towards 'ending' Nathan always avoided fixing them. In the penultimate session, by which time he knew the date for starting at his mainstream school, he was debating whether he would take home *Colourful Beauty* when his 'time' finished. He decided to dictate some more of his story. It ran: '*Colourful Beauty* filled up with coal, enough to get to school. She got to school and had a snack and he did a lot of work and he had his lunch at school. The children wanted a ride and she took them all round the playground, and went home on the school bus.' (Nathan's previous response when asked to write had been tantrums and weeping, and fearful, tentative meaningless marks on the page. It was easy to see the direction his thoughts had taken and his developing belief in his potential survival in mainstream school.) When asked if the train took the bus because it had no wheels, he looked surprised, saying, 'It won't get far like that.' Twenty wheels were rapidly fixed on, painted in different colours, and the completed model was dazzling. Nathan wondered if he should leave it with me or take it home. Not wanting to deprive him of it, nor give him the impression that I did not want it, I suggested taking a photograph and this impressed Nathan as much as it seemed to relieve him.

The format of the last session was as usual, and acknowledged by us both as the final one. Nathan acquitted himself well, although he fell off his chair several times. The session was held at a time that was earlier than usual, so that there could be a party for him in the classroom, before he went home. He recalled aloud another session that had to be held early – 'I was cross with you for that.'

Conclusion

The quotes in the introduction would imply that when a young child, or a baby, loses a sibling, they are not experiencing the loss of that sibling but, rather, the mother's reaction to the death of her child. In the light of this it is possible to suggest that Nathan's problems and ambivalences came out of his mother's emotional unavailability at birth and ongoing infancy. It would appear that one response by mother to her little daughter's death is still to cram the day with work. Perhaps she feels she cannot risk getting too close to her surviving children. Much of Nathan's day was spent away from his mother and, when she did make time for him, she found him, even though he was now a schoolchild, 'cold and unresponsive'. 'What is apparent is that if the adult is to have any effect on the child, it is essential that she must be closely attuned to that child – she must be highly sensitive of the child's abilities, interests, and skills as they unfold themselves from one moment to the next' (Schaffer, 1990)

Information on Nathan's family background was not readily available, and not much is known about the first child. Drake reports, 'Some children will act out elaborate games of make-believe in order to convince themselves that the person who has died is not dead . . . it is this situation which can so readily follow on from a death, where all the facts are not made available' (Drake, 1991). Similarly, much of Nathan's confusion stems from what he does not know, or thinks he should not know. 'Parents teach their children to behave in particular ways, both by what they tell them to do (precept) and by what the child observes of the parents own ways of behaving (percept)' (Rutter, 1975).

Nathan's guilt and anxiety may have been close to Klein's definition of envy: 'Envy is the angry feeling that another person possesses and enjoys something desirable – the envious impulse being to take it away or spoil it. Envy implies the subject's relation to one person only, and goes back to the earliest exclusive relationship with the mother.' She suggests also that a child's unconscious envy puts . . . ' the bad parts of the self into the mother, primarily her breast, to spoil and destroy her; in the deepest sense this means destroying her creativeness' (Klein, 1957). To take her view, if a child envies a dead sibling and wishes it dead they may feel that they have killed it. In the same way, Nathan was very afraid of his hateful feelings towards his younger sister, possibly feeling they would bring about her death. Guilty feelings at being glad that a rival has been removed are added to guilt and remorse at having killed the rival. Beaumont, when working with a young adolescent girl whose mother had given birth to a stillborn child, observed,

It seems to me that the 'remaining member' can feel guilty without occupying the place of the lost person. She has therefore, to limit her achievements and spoil her space both to assuage her guilt and also to guard against retribution from the dead person. As a replacement child, she also seems to feel guilty about being alive at all and about the possibility of enjoying herself. She has to make her whole existence unbearable to prevent herself from being envied by the stillborn child (Beaumont, 1988).

When his sister died, Nathan was in what Stern calls 'the period of the emergent self', that is, 'a sense of the emergent self is the process of coming into being' (Stern, 1985). At that time he was receiving many confusing messages from his parents; their sadness because his sister had died, pleasure at his birth, disappointment that he did not feed, and in addition he experienced maternal unavailability. As he grew older, it seems he developed a sense of being someone else, or rather, being the wrong person. His desire to be a girl (shown by his dressing in a frilly dress), a baby ('Wead dis one to Nafun'), and his determination to be first, suggest that he wanted to replace his dead sister. It seems feasible to extend this thinking to Nathan's probable desire to please his mother by restoring this lost child to her.

The hurt he experienced at his mother's emotional withdrawal, and later her physical absence, found expression in his seeking to punish her by seizing power from her, disobeying and belittling her, being unable to separate from her, and having fantasies of her as omnipotent, beautiful and exclusively his. This state of affairs is very different from Winnicott's statement when he asserts, 'The child comes to love and hate simultaneously, and to accept the contradiction' (Winnicott, 1965).

My brief work with Nathan could not eliminate the inevitable recurrence of painful feelings, but it provided him as an individual with new resources to confront the pain, and instil some confidence in an image of self as accepted, and capable. Being read to, and learning to read, seemed to help Nathan to think about previously unthinkable thoughts, which brought about change in his views and attitudes. Barrett and Trevitt aver:

> The anger, frustration and misery that previously accompanied learning can now be examined and recognised, and in due course, acknowledged and owned. Previously uncontrolled letters and numbers can now be placed and recorded where the children choose, and they can see that order makes sense to themselves and others. Eventually, they recognise that feelings, too, can be controlled (Barrett and Trevitt, 1991).

Comments on Educational Therapy in the Classroom

To bring the techniques of educational therapy into the classroom, the normal, interactive environment in which the teacher, or as in my case the classroom assistant, can be as daunting as it can be rewarding.

Should a teacher decide to bring education therapy into the class, after training, studying and developing a therapeutic mindset, there are some factors that will strongly influence its success. One of these is the availability of support from well-established educational therapists. Another is the need to examine and reassess what feelings the teacher brings to the classroom, and her reactions to the children's material. Sometimes working with a child in the therapeutic situation arouses painful feelings or anger in the teacher; or these can be the feelings that have arisen in the child, who, finding them unbearable, has projected them on to the teacher. This process, called transference, offers the children a chance to see these strong feelings managed, and to know they can be survived. If the teacher is not aware of this, and consequently cannot think the issue through, her reaction may stop the therapeutic process, dead-ending any thinking about an uncomfortable issue.

Just the actuality of a child attending educational therapy sessions, away from the classroom, can engender reactions ranging from mild resentment to outright hostility among school staff. It is difficult to explain to colleagues a new way of thinking about, and interacting with, children whose behaviour has placed them in special units. There is a danger that misunderstandings can undermine the teacher undertaking a more therapeutic approach. It might be reasonable to suggest that an introduction to educational therapy be incorporated into teacher training, with opportunities to carry out some focused work with a child (but not without supervision). Protests that educational therapy is unfair on the rest of the class, is time-consuming and has no guarantee of success, can just as easily be levelled at behaviour modification, which some teachers find more acceptable. Another possible area of resistance can be the teacher having to give up 'not knowing'; it can be very painful for the teacher having to acknowledge unbearable feelings (see also chapter 7).

On a practical level a school may find it difficult to provide a space for the work to be carried out; or there may be resentment at the interruption to the timetable. Progress is often slow and the child's pleasure on leaving the class may make the teacher feel that what she has to offer the child is not good enough. The feeling that the therapist is having an easy time may be prevalent. The school staff, under pressure themselves, often find it difficult, having survived a challenging lesson, to accept that their more expert colleague has 'only been teaching one child'. Therapy may be perceived by non-involved staff as having a kind of mystique; this is sometimes reproduced in the environment and seen in the mysterious double-booking of rooms, disappearance of materials, or unreported absences of the pupil concerned. If therapy is held in sufficiently low regard, and looked on as being 'only playing and talking', then the space reluctantly provided can be subjected to interruptions; a room crammed with old furniture and fittings; or a music room, lined with dozens of tempting, jangling instruments. If not these, then it will be a cupboard or store. Even if a member of staff is willing to explore therapy, two fears may prevent them from introducing it into their class: bringing out painful feelings in the child, and dealing with the painful feelings engendered in themselves. The value of supervision during training can be seen in my work with Nathan, but this 'different' experience too can be misunderstood by colleagues.

As therapeutic techniques are introduced in the classroom, many of the objections and attitudes lose their validity. Not every child in the class will require in-depth educational therapy, but a psycho-dynamic approach and a deeper understanding of all interactive behaviour will surely contribute to more 'successful' teaching and learning.

Chapter 10
Working and Learning with a Vulnerable Adolescent

DAVID SHOTT

Working in a School for Young People with Emotional and Behavioural Difficulties

For some 15 years I have been working in a residential special school with young people suffering from a range of emotional, behavioural and educational difficulties. Here I shall attempt to demonstrate how I have been able to reassess some previously held assumptions about adolescent behaviour in the class, through my own learning, while interacting with an individual youngster in weekly educational therapy sessions.

For the young people referred to my school there are clear and regular indicators that they have failed to cope with the system that is provided within mainstream education. Time and time again, phrases such as 'displays inappropriate behaviour', 'disruptive in the classroom', 'abusive towards adults', 'shows little or no self-control', 'lacks concentration', 'restless, uninterested, withdrawn in class', 'has a low level of self-esteem', and 'incapable of forming relationships' appear on their statements of special educational needs.

Staff and pupils of a large mainstream school have to tolerate and deal with the regular outbursts of attention-seeking, aggressive and abusive behaviour of disruptive pupils. Any school has a responsibility to all its pupils and a duty to ensure that the learning process be allowed to flow with the minimal amount of chaos. Inevitably, highly disruptive pupils do not or cannot accept the additional help and support that is offered and seem unable to change their patterns of behaviour. Frequently for a boy like Joseph, this can lead to permanent exclusion from the school.

Joseph's Story

Joseph, an active and robust eight-year-old who lived with his mother and two elder brothers, was first brought to the attention of the County

153

Psychological Service in 1989. His name was raised at a local support group meeting due to concerns about his poor concentration in the classroom and his inability to conform to the school's code of behaviour. He was unable even to sit in one place during any of his lessons. In 1990, after Joseph was transferred to another primary school in order to give him a fresh start, the educational psychologist at the time worked with his class teacher to set up a behaviour modification system. A child psychiatrist from the Child and Family Guidance Service saw Joseph and his mother in weekly family therapy sessions in order to try and support their relationship which was becoming increasingly fragile.

Two years later Joseph was again referred to the Psychological Service as a consequence of Social Service concerns about his behaviour at home. Joseph's mother felt that he was beyond her control. He would not conform to established boundaries which she tried to set, he was extremely manipulative and rude and was stealing money and cigarettes. He would frequently leave the house for lengthy periods of time without consulting his mother and was known to be associating with a group of youths considerably older than him and well known to the local police. His previously upsetting school-based behaviour was now largely contained at his second primary school although it remained difficult to motivate Joseph to produce any work. A very different concern now arose in school. Joseph's behaviour became sexualised and was particularly noticeable towards female members of staff.

When Joseph transferred to the local comprehensive school he again began to create enormous difficulties in a number of lessons. He frequently resorted to attention-seeking behaviour such as leaving his seat and wandering around the room, calling out during lessons, using foul and abusive language in order to provoke other pupils and members of staff, throwing objects at other pupils, and refusing to leave the room when requested. He continued to exhibit extremely low levels of concentration and towards the end of his first term, staff at the school were finding it more and more difficult to cope with any of Joseph's behaviour. Their concern increased with regard to the frequent episodes of Joseph's crude sexualised behaviour being exhibited within the classroom setting. Joseph's mother had been kept informed of these problems throughout this time and had worked cooperatively with the school to try to get to the root of such behaviour.

Unfortunately, by the end of this first term Joseph had to be permanently excluded from this school. He received three hours a week home tuition at this time pending a possible transfer to a new mainstream school. The home tuition was quite successful as Joseph related well to his home tutor, but he soon began to get bored with so much free time on his hands. The area exclusions panel decided that Joseph should be placed in an alternative mainstream comprehensive school.

Serious problems continued after this transfer and formal assessment proceedings were initiated during Joseph's first year at his new school. In January 1994 a Statement of Special Educational Needs was issued by the local authority which recognised Joseph's emotional and behavioural difficulties and which recommended a placement at a specialist residential school. Although Joseph's difficulties were very real, he was not the only one: I could also have been talking about a boy called Tom, Robert, Michael, David or Jamie.

If parents, teachers, representatives of the Area Psychological Service and any other agencies involved such as the Health Authority and Social Services are in agreement that ordinary schooling is no longer possible or appropriate, then a young person like Joseph may be referred to a school such as mine catering for adolescents suffering from a range of emotional, behavioural and educational difficulties. It is in this small school environment that the young person can continue to have full access to the National Curriculum, while experiencing a high adult: pupil ratio, a consistent and structured environment which can help him to understand any consequences of his behaviour through a positive behaviour management programme, social skills training, support for his learning difficulties, a 24-hour curriculum with the opportunity to participate in structured extra-curricular activities and have close adult supervision.

Within this type of small school environment, one can attempt to begin to interpret how the young person is really feeling. It becomes clear over a period of time that our young people are anxious, uncertain, confused, angry, out of control and as such are, of course, feeling highly vulnerable. They have often expressed these feelings thus far in their lives through negative defensive strategies. As an experienced teacher working with youngsters with emotional and behavioural difficulties, I have learned, over a period of many years, that in order to work positively and productively with this client group, certain conditions have to prevail.

As I worked I gradually became aware that I was able to meet many of the emotional needs of these special youngsters by providing them with care, understanding, tolerance, firmness, fairness and calmness. I certainly discovered a good deal about myself through my work with disturbed children as I began to be able to peel back the unattractive exteriors that many of these children presented to the world; in the process revealing their hidden anxieties and inner desperation. Time and time again I asked myself and other members of the staff why children become like this. Our answers were perhaps predictable. 'Oh, he's from a broken home you know.' 'We think he might be abused.' 'Have you met his parents? Then you'll know why.'

These standard answers that were put forward provided me with an excuse or reason not to question further. They had to satisfy me at the time, as the hurly-burly routine of a special school did not really allow sufficient time for further questioning. However, when I began my educational therapy diploma training, I was able to reassess my knowledge of the fundamental reasons for disturbed behaviour in children. It was an opportunity to re-examine many of my previously held assumptions about adolescent behaviour. Some of the theories introduced as part of my diploma training afforded me the opportunity to evaluate and make use of concepts such as, 'the secure base' (Ainsworth, 1967) 'attachment and loss' (Bowlby, 1969, 1973, 1980), 'educational attachment figure' (Barrett and Trevitt, 1991), 'holding' (Winnicott, 1971) and 'good enough experiences' (Winnicott, 1965).

I began to re-examine why the young people with whom I work might be behaving in the way that they do, why they sometimes act in such a bizarre and seemingly irrational manner and why they convince themselves that they are worthless and that what they manage to produce is rubbish. I questioned too why they often continue to alienate themselves from adults by living up to their past reputations and by regularly testing both the tolerance and also the resolve of those adults working with them. After lectures and seminars which focused on the theory behind the various concepts that I have mentioned above, and while continuing to benefit from regular group supervision sessions, I began working and learning with a vulnerable adolescent in my own school, through weekly educational therapy sessions.

Mark and his Family Members

Mark was referred to my school when he was 11 years of age. He was quite an attractive looking boy (with fair hair and a healthy complexion), but the thing I noticed most about him was that he rarely smiled or indeed showed any range of emotions. I knew that he was a member of a large scattered family and this made me think about how an enforced separation from a large number of his relations might be affecting his behaviour in school. Prior to moving to the area in which I work, with his mother and elder stepsister, Mark had lived in an inner-city area. He had two other grown-up stepbrothers, one of whom lived in the South East of England; the other one had moved abroad. The remainder of his relatives, including his maternal grandparents, continued to live a considerable distance away from him and I discovered he now had little contact with them. His father had left home when Mark was only 18 months old, and it seemed that Mark had seen very little of his father since that time.

I was able to arrange a very productive meeting with Mark's mother during which she told me that she had been through two unhappy marriages and had been very anxious about raising Mark in an inner-city area. Consequently it was her desire to protect her son that had prompted the move that had led to his family becoming more scattered.

I felt that Mark still greatly resented this move and I suspected it had set off in him feelings of having no control over his own life. Mark's mother told me that the elder three children, stepbrothers and sister, were now adults themselves with their own independent lives to lead. (I asked myself whether this mother was perhaps being so possessive and over-protective of her youngest child in order to try to combat her own feelings of abandonment by other family members.) As she continued to speak I wondered too whether she could not face up to the prospect of Mark growing up and abandoning her – in reality Mark had probably felt abandoned by her and the rest of his scattered family for many years. Perhaps by seeking from Mark the love that she had desperately sought and failed to find within her own relationships, she was inverting the normal parent – child relationship, and although it might have appeared that Mark was being over-indulged, in fact he was probably struggling under the very heavy burden placed on him by his mother. Under such intense pressure from his main care-giver, I began to think that it was hardly surprising that Mark had been unable either to sustain age-appropriate behaviour nor to develop normal friendships in the school setting as he embarked upon the uncertainties of adolescence.

Following what I experienced as an unburdening of many feelings from her past, Mark's mother, I felt, readily agreed to my offer of one-to-one work with Mark for a limited period.

Anton Obholzer (1992) suggests that if a child has had a 'good enough' (Winnicott, 1965) experience of the world and is able to relate to and love others, then he will 'embark on the opportunities and stresses of adolescence to enrich his inner world and to lay the foundations for adult functioning'. He goes on to say that the 'deprived child' will also have the chance 'to re-enact his deprived state of mind and way of relating'. If he is lucky he may be offered a different response and consequently he may have the opportunity to reconsider his earlier view of life. I hoped that my one-to-one work with Mark, using our educational therapeutic approach, might offer him a different response.

My feeling was that Mark was in many ways 'a deprived child' as described by Obholzer, but that he could be helped to change his way of relating to others. I felt his mother cared enough to respond to our concern and express her own, but I guessed his anger towards family members whose absence prevented any hope of having a relationship, plus the lack of managing any relationships in school, had led to his view of himself to be currently 'bad'.

Educational psychologist's report

Problems had been noted from Mark's early days when he attended a nursery school. He had shown aggressive behaviour towards other children, was unable to share toys and books and demanded exclusive attention from the nursery teacher. Therefore his mother was forced to remove him because of the high level of disruption that he was regularly causing. He experienced similar problems when he began school and these difficulties continued to haunt him even after he and his mother moved away from the inner-city environment.

School report

As stated previously, Mark was eventually transferred to my school when he was 11 years old. Although he initially settled in quite well, as he began to approach adolescence a number of teachers became increasingly concerned about Mark's behaviour and lack of achievement in class. His form tutor, an experienced and popular member of staff, expressed her concern that he had poor literacy skills, a minimal concentration span and inability to pick up new topics. She commented also about his very poor relationships with his classmates, and that his behaviour in class was becoming more and more inappropriate and challenging, particularly his use of foul language aimed at her and also at his peers.

Preparation for working with Mark

When I began my educational therapy sessions with Mark it was my real hope that through a 'second-chance' learning experience (Barrett and Trevitt, 1991) he would begin to improve his cognitive skills and develop an ability to understand, tolerate and manage the changes that had happened to him during his life thus far, and relate them to those that he would have to face up to in the future.

Prior to our first session, I established an initial meeting with Mark in the room that I had already earmarked for our regular use. I collected Mark from his classroom and we walked together across the playground and into the residential part of the school. Mark was quite relaxed as he entered the room and I offered him a seat next to me. I told him that I would like to spend some special time with him on a weekly basis to try to help him with some of the things that he was currently finding quite difficult. I suggested that he was currently finding difficulty with reading, writing and spelling; that his poor behaviour in the classroom was causing him, his teachers and his peers a lot of problems. Mark did not try to deny that he had difficulties and actually agreed that his current behaviour was causing him a good deal of concern because he did not know how to change it. I told Mark that I had already contacted his mother and had asked her permission to work with him and that she had given her approval. We agreed to meet at the same time on the same day each week for a period of 10 weeks and I explained to him that we would always meet in the room that we were in now as it was warm and quiet and somewhere, hopefully, we would not be disturbed. (The focus on thinking about Mark as an individual made me realise that in the past, however well I had prepared the curriculum for a class, I had rarely found time to think about each child's needs and feelings.)

I explained to Mark that we would always start and finish our sessions on time and that I would let him know when we were coming towards the end of any session so that we could both prepare ourselves for the ending of that session. (This reinforced my realisation that preparing individuals for the ending of class lessons should be given similar emphasis in the classroom; something which, as a busy class teacher, it is easy to forget.)

I also told Mark that he would have exclusive use of a box containing educational and play equipment such as card, crayons, string, paper, scissors, felt-tips, pencils, eraser, playing cards, dice and farm animals and that I would keep this safely for him between our sessions. I hoped that he would realise that my message to him was that, by keeping his box safely between each session, I would also be keeping him in mind.

Mark seemed quite happy with these arrangements as he told me that he was looking forward to discovering what would be in his box when he came to our first session next week. (I felt he had already begun to differentiate sessions from lessons.)

The first session

I collected Mark from his classroom and we crossed the playground together. Mark asked me what we would be doing and I told him that I would explain things when we got to our room. I had been fortunate in obtaining a quiet, bright, spacious room with a warm atmosphere, and with lots of stimulating pictures on the wall, in the residential part of the school. As our sessions progressed, I began to learn how important the setting was if these sessions were to be successful. I discovered that noise, distractions and the occasional accidental interruptions could have serious effects on the quality of the session. I asked myself if similar distractions were therefore major reasons for disruption in the classroom situation. So many thoughts flooded through my mind and yet I felt I had to ensure, somehow, that I kept a space in my mind for Mark.

Mark sat down next to me and I reminded him of our initial meeting and the aims that we had established for our time together. He eagerly opened his box and asked if he could keep it. I reinforced the fact that it was for his exclusive use during our sessions but that I would keep it safe during the week. Having established a clear principle that we had learned in our own training sessions, I pressed on with a little more confidence. I asked Mark if he would like to use some of the materials in his box, and with a little encouragement he began to draw a picture of his home and family.

Afterwards, as I wrote up my notes, I felt that things had gone very well for my first session. In retrospect, I feel certain now that the session was very much 'stage managed' by myself. I had set out with the aim of getting Mark to do certain tasks. For example I wanted him to start drawing a picture of his family whether he liked it or not. The picture that Mark drew of his home and his family I felt might be saying a great deal about Mark's image of himself and his relationship with his attachment figures. However, I had in fact, at the time, evaluated the success of the session against what Mark had produced on paper. As I have gained more experience through further sessions with Mark and other youngsters, I have put a far greater emphasis on the importance of being able to listen so as to 'hear' more than is actually being said. This is such an important skill to develop, and it brings to mind Francis Dale's (1992) thoughts regarding communicating with vulnerable children, when he poses the question, 'Are you really hearing what the child has to tell you?' One child in care spoke for many children when he said: 'Adults listen to us but don't hear us.'

I feel I must also mention here that the occasion that appeared to cause Mark most anguish in our first session was when he drew himself in his family picture. He drew himself as a small and seemingly isolated member of his family and, as he drew, he shuffled uncomfortably in his chair. As he finished drawing himself, he searched for the eraser in his box, erased himself and then drew himself again, a rather forlorn figure, lonely, isolated and, in his own eyes, an insignificant little boy in the midst of his scattered family.

When Mark had left the room to return to his classroom I sat and reflected. It became my real hope that what I was beginning to discover about my own learning through supervision and through my interaction with Mark, I would be able to put to use in the classroom situation with other learning-disabled adolescents.

Further sessions with Mark

During my weekly sessions with Mark I was able to make a number of observations. It became clear to me that he felt deep anger and resentment that he had been forced to leave most of his family in the inner city in order to move away at his mother's instigation.

Prior to our third session and due to an unforeseen emergency at school, I had to rearrange my time for meeting Mark. I saw him in the morning and explained why it was necessary to change the time of our session. Initially Mark accepted this but when I went to collect him from his classroom he was very reluctant to come. He complained that the other members of his class had a free lesson since their regular teacher was away. I reiterated to Mark that I was sorry for the disruption caused but that it was beyond my control; he somewhat reluctantly accepted this situation and we made our way across to our regular room in silence.

Mark sat down and continued to tell me that he wished that his mum had not given me permission to work with him and that he was going to make his mum change her mind because what we were doing was boring and that he did not want to come to any more sessions. I was aware that I felt irritated by this but remained calm and understanding. I told Mark that I could not force him to come to these sessions as they were voluntary, but that since we had agreed to work together for 10 sessions I would be keeping my side of the bargain.

He went on to say that he hated where he was now living and wished that he could return to the inner-city area from which he had moved. He also complained that he had not been consulted about the move. (It would have been helpful if I could have made use of this remark to refer to his not being consulted about our change of time also.) I suggested that this was probably the cause of some of his anger. He implied that he didn't know, then sat quietly for a while, thinking, before telling me 'yes,' this was one of the reasons why he felt angry. I told Mark that I had felt sad, angry and somewhat frightened when, as a boy of his age, my family had moved and I had ended up in a new school having left all my friends behind. At this point Mark seemed visibly calmer and began to relax a little. I wondered whether he felt that I had been able to contain his feelings of anger and frustration safely without reacting negatively and that this was reassuring to him. I had acknowledged his reasons for feeling angry and explained to him that, because I understood why he felt angry, I would not become angry with him. He had consciously or unconsciously tested me to see whether I was able to contain his anger and anxiety and I felt that this interactive was a significant factor in our ongoing relationship.

During the next session Mark suddenly decided to tell me that he liked where he was living now. I gently reminded him that last week he had told me that he hated where he lived and wished that he could return to the inner city. He replied that he did not really hate where he lived but that he missed the excitement and hustle and bustle of the big city.

After the session on reflection I could see that Mark had probably been trying to tell me that, since he felt that he had no choice in determining his own life (including our session time), then he could accept no responsibility for his own behaviour and actions. He would not, or could not, be held accountable. This feeling was confirmed for me by the writing of Barrett and Trevitt when they state, 'Most of the children referred to us for educational therapy feel that they have no control over circumstances concerning themselves and their families. They do not perceive themselves as individuals who have a choice' (Barrett and Trevitt, 1991). Mark's behaviour made me feel that he could certainly fit into this category.

Mark's relationship with this mother

The theme of Mark's relationship with his mother was one that prevailed throughout our sessions. In the very first one, when Mark was drawing a picture of his house, I noticed that the only room that was drawn in any detail was his mother's bedroom. This room had a very cosy image with lots of potted plants lining the window sills and the family cat lazing in the sunshine that streamed into the room. In a later session Mark confirmed that he would like to be this cat and I shall return to this point later in the chapter. I felt at the time that Mark was indicating that he was still anxious and uncertain about his relationship with his mother and that what he had really desired was a close, warm relationship that I guessed he had probably not experienced for some, at least, of his early years. From other sessions, however, it became clear to me that Mark had suffered more recently from a degree of maternal over-protection. As we worked together I sensed that his feelings towards his mother fluctuated between intense love and anger bordering on hatred for the way in which, from Mark's viewpoint, she had failed to satisfy his earliest needs and yet now smothered him with the sort of mothering that he neither desired nor needed as an adolescent. I did not voice these thoughts in my time with Mark.

This love–hate relationship that Mark appeared to project towards his mother was exemplified during one particular session when we were concentrating on a spelling exercise. Working on a 'scattered family' theme, I had taken a number of words relating to members of the family, such as mother, father, brother, sister, grandfather and so on, cut each word up into its individual letters and mixed the letters around in a random fashion. I presented Mark with the task of remaking any family words that he could piece together. The first word that he spelled was 'Shit' followed by the word 'Mother'. Whether this had been done consciously or unconsciously, it suggested to me that there was a good deal of seething anger and frustration within Mark which, perhaps through our sessions, he was beginning to be able to direct more appropriately into his learning; in this case, into his spellings.

On another occasion, Mark had brought along his family photograph album to show me. I remember quite clearly that Mark flicked through the pages before I had really had time to ask any questions which, in retrospect, he may have found too painful to answer.

Did Mark feel 'held in mind' by any of the figures in the photograph album? I asked myself this question, and concluded that he probably did not. After all, had he not been either taken away from what I imagined might have been his attachment figures or had he not seen them withdraw themselves from him? In fact, it would appear that Mark continued to be 'anxiously attached' (Bowlby, 1969) to his mother. Since he was just over one year old he had had no father to hold him physically or to hold him in mind, and, following the move from an inner city, he no longer felt held by those with whom he may well have formed strong positive attachments.

Bowlby (1988) states, 'Should a child's care givers actively reject him, he is likely to develop a pattern of behaviour in which angry behaviour is apt to become prominent.' Mark's angry behaviour had certainly become prominent from when he was a little boy and had continued to feature in his development through to adolescence. He seemed to have followed a continuing downward spiral demonstrated by his behaviour in the school setting. Was this behaviour reflecting the fear, bewilderment and anxiety that I thought Mark undoubtedly had felt as he struggled from one new situation to another?

Now that Mark was being afforded the opportunity of 'second-chance' learning through individual educational therapy sessions and had clearly used this opportunity to off-load some of his feelings, I wondered whether there could be any significant changes in his behaviour in and outside the classroom. Although his attitude to completing tasks with me had improved, I felt it was important that he still felt 'held' by other staff members when our work together had ended.

Developing a 'Whole School' Approach to Meeting Mark's Needs and Managing his Behaviour

Like so many others within my school, Mark was only one of many whose learning and behaviour indicated their distress. He had frequently caused considerable anxiety, distress and frustration among his teachers and carers. He had often behaved in a manner that seemed intended to shock and upset those adults who were attempting to work with him. His mother had not been able to withstand his aggression and anxiety when he was a young child and I felt it was now of vital importance that he encountered adults who could tolerate but also help him to manage this destructive element of his nature. Mark needed to know, and to feel safe in the knowledge, that there were adults who could accept him as a person and at the same time contain his feelings of anxiety, aggression and despair.

Both Mark and I knew that my intervention would have to be a limited one. I therefore arranged for time to talk about Mark and the feelings that he engendered in people at one of our weekly staff meetings. A number of people were very quick to voice their opinions and a fairly clear picture was painted. Mark was causing considerable disruption in class and also in the care setting and most people were finding him very difficult to work with. On a positive note, however, most of the adults who worked with Mark stated that they felt he had a very likeable side to his character and that they did not wish to reject him, but needed strategies for dealing with the regular disruption that he caused.

After a lengthy discussion we agreed a short-term action plan, the essence of which was to reinforce, accentuate and reward any positive periods of behaviour while challenging and dealing appropriately with the negative aspects of it. Mark would spend time with his form tutor on a daily basis to celebrate the successes of the day while discussing the failures and looking at ways in which they might have been avoided. Secondly, we agreed to allocate to Mark as much in-class support as possible during the school day. Thirdly, all members of staff would immediately challenge Mark's use of inappropriate language, show their disapproval at the time but follow up any such episodes by seeing Mark privately, later that day, in order to reinforce the fact that he was still valued and to try to show him that he did not need to use such language. It was also agreed that all incidents of positive or negative behaviour and achievement would be recorded within the main daily communication system and that Mark would be seen by me (in my new role as acting-head) on a weekly basis to review his progress.

We have all endeavoured to encourage Mark to internalise good feelings about himself and have attempted to increase his own desire to change a negative pattern of behaviour and learning towards a more positive one. At the same time he continues his struggle with the conflicts of adolescence.

Conclusions

During the time that I was working with Mark I started to piece together an intricate and complex jigsaw that would ultimately help me to understand at least some of the reasons for Mark's learning disabilities. Through my own learning opportunities I was able to gain a better insight into the inner turmoil of a vulnerable adolescent, struggling to come to terms with himself as an individual and his relationship with his mother, his peer group, the care and teaching staff, and his unavailable family members.

My experiences with Mark helped me to see how his young life had been plagued with anxiety, uncertainty, instability and pain, to which he drew attention by his inappropriate behaviour. The work has also helped me to think about the reasons why so many other youngsters in my school act in anger, treating us, the adults, with suspicion and mistrust, often appearing reluctant to confide in anybody with their problems. I began to learn that we, as adults, very often do not hear what young people are saying to us; that we have a responsibility to improve our listening skills in order to allow the adolescents in our care to be heard.

When Mark had told me, in one of our early sessions, that he would have liked to have taken the place of the family cat on his mother's bedroom window sill, had I really heard what he was saying to me, and if so, why did I not develop this opportunity of working within the metaphor? It was clearly to do with my own inexperience, and it was only during one of my supervision sessions that my tutor helped me to understand how I had missed this golden opportunity of working within the metaphor, by asking about the cat's feelings. If I could have turned back the clock I would have developed this theme with Mark, but I was learning too, and am now able to value working with metaphors and have a better understanding of the significance of symbols.

Chapter 12
Educational Therapy with a Learning-disabled Adult

MARIANNE STURTRIDGE

An exploration of the Application of Educational Therapy Techniques While Working with Learning-disabled Adults

I am employed as a lecturer in Special Educational Needs and creative arts at a College of Further Education in the south-west of England. I teach adults whose ages range from 20 to 50 years. Their ability level varies from total dependence to being able to travel and shop independently.

Most of my students live in residential homes where they have limited choice and opportunity in making decisions related to their own lives. This is demonstrated by the compliance, low motivation and feelings of powerlessness that they bring to the classroom. I use the skills I have in art which I find an invaluable aid when I cannot reach a student, or am attempting to help them to communicate their frustrations. My diploma training in educational therapy allows me to explore possible reasons for my students' learning problems, as well as providing me with resources to make tasks enjoyable.

With all adults who are functioning at a low level of maturity I attempt to find a starting point to bridge the gaps between their learning blocks and their potential. The students' greatest disability, I believe, is their feeling of not being in control of their lives coupled with not having someone who thinks of them in a special way. As a teacher I can feel at a loss when faced with concerns relating to students' social or emotional well-being that are outside the classroom situation. I use my art and an educational therapy approach to address these concerns. Osborne and Barrett (1985) define this intervention as, '. . . a therapeutic approach which takes into account the emotional as well as the cognitive aspects of learning.'

I shall refer briefly to Arthur but the main focus of the work is on my attempts to understand Martha, a 24-year-old female student with learning difficulties. She was a member of my class prior to our one-to-one work. I was frustrated with her grunts and monosyllabic pattern of speech. After several attempts where I applied 'taught' methods to encourage Martha to speak in sentences, I turned, in my state of desperation, to drawing as a means of communication. I incorporated educational therapy techniques with my training in special education and creativity to communicate with Martha. This reduced the strain for Martha when she did not want to talk and made me feel less incompetent as a teacher working therapeutically. The need to establish boundaries between my roles as class teacher and a student of educational therapy was difficult but necessary for classroom management. When working with adults who are functioning at a concrete or primary school stage in learning, a teacher can feel overwhelmed by a need to provide a social experience and attempt to address the emotional needs of the learner while relating this to their different level of cognitive stage of functioning.

Arthur

My classroom observations of Arthur, a 20-year-old, who, with his assured manner and handsome appearance, looked out of place in a group with learning difficulties. (He revealed a darker, tormented side when I started working on a one-to-one hourly basis with him in an attempt to provide a space for him in which to think about his painful thoughts.) Arthur's constant demands on the teachers by way of verbal abuse to other students or periods of withdrawal from learning could not be met within a group situation. The one-to-one sessions were viewed by me as a solution to improving my classroom management while providing Arthur with 'space' to think in order that we might explore why he did not seem able to learn in a group. Arthur did not join in class activities but he made fun of another student constantly during the lessons. He was always the last to leave the classroom. When I suggested that we might spend time outside class working on his reading, he gladly accepted as he felt this was the cause of all his other problems.

When Arthur's term at college ended he was due to return to a sheltered workshop for disabled adults. He disliked the other trainees, calling them 'spastics'. Such workshops or centres are under the control of the social services. They provide training in horticulture, sorting and packing small items for factories (as contract work), work placements in industry, as well as the opportunity to attend the local College of Further Education. Here they have a syllabus of basic literacy, numeracy and training in life-skills. (In order to ensure funding for programmes of learning for such adults it is necessary for us to show the adult's academic achievements. This can create anxiety for the teacher who feels under pressure to adopt a formal teaching style and deliver a syllabus that does not allow space to think about why the students cannot always retain the information they are given.)

In my sessions with Arthur we considered what would make learning easier for him, why he thought he could not manage learning, and what part this played in his relationships to his peer group and others. While not sharing his view that being able to read would solve his problems, Rourke and Feurst's (1991) research with adults who are learning-disabled shows the cumulative disadvantages for those who are unable to learn. They state: 'Indeed, it is a commonly held notion that persons who experience significant difficulties in learning are most definitely susceptible to disorders in other areas of human functioning, such as the "emotional" and "social" dimensions of life.'

I felt that while Arthur was preoccupied with trying to make sense of his past, a history of changing residential homes and schools, there was no space in his mind for 'holding' information. Trower et al. (1978) quote Rotter and Lefcroft's research with people living in mental institutions, where they examined the responses of the inmates to their environment. It appeared that they could be divided into those who were 'in control' of their situations and those 'being controlled' by their environments.

Arthur placed great emphasis on understanding the world, knowing himself and the feelings of others. He was frightened of committing himself to writing that was never good enough; the same was true of reading. Arthur was acutely aware of the handicap but could not allow himself to learn. He described it: 'It's like knives coming towards you, they never stop.' This statement made me feel sad and helpless but I thought his autocentric approach was preventing learning, tolerance of others and ability to externalise his thinking.

To illustrate ways of channelling thoughts in directions other than himself, I introduced subjects that Arthur might enjoy. He responded positively, saying he was 'fed up' with all the bad thoughts going through his mind, which he could not stop. We agreed we could try to make some sense of his thoughts. I started using a spider diagram while talking about my difficulty with writing. Arthur appeared to collaborate and seemed to understand my difficulty. He then produced a piece on expressing feelings (see Figure 12.1).

It felt good to see some of the enormous sadness lift from Arthur who appeared to become a happy, eager-to-please child. However, I imagined that I was now responsible for Arthur's thoughts and this caused anxiety within me. I could not disappoint Arthur, otherwise I would be continuing his pattern of rejections. I wondered if his inconsistency in remembering related to his unsettled lifestyle. His apparent inability to retain information puzzled him and was a cause of annoyance for teachers who felt exasperated by their time and efforts at teaching him unsuccessfully. Arthur was receptive when he was receiving one-to-one teaching, and later reflection indicated that it was individual attention that Arthur most craved.

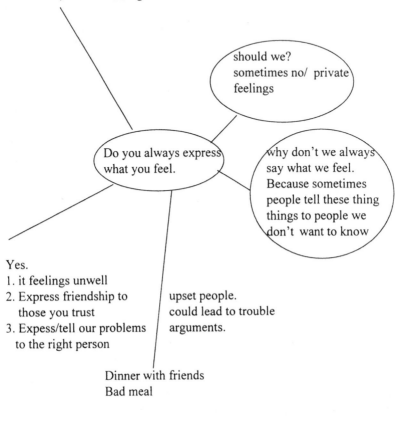

Figure 12.1 Arthur's 'Feelings'.

When I spoke to another teacher she was not aware of his spiteful behaviour towards others in the group or his constant demands on the teacher's attention. Was this because an acknowledgement of his tyrannical behaviour to quiet students would create extra work or bring to the surface problems that were unmanageable for the teacher? I connected Arthur's not knowing who he was with his feeling of rejection by others, which he had experienced in the past. His conflict with authority figures resulted in him losing a work placement, thus self-inflicting further rejection. Winnicott (1971) illustrates the need for continuity in a child's life and the disabling effect of constant change on emotional and cognitive development. 'Continuity of care has become a central feature of the concept of the facilitating environment. The new baby in dependence must have a continuity in the line of his or her life, not a pattern of reacting to the unpredicted and for ever starting again' (Winnicott, 1971).

The following extract was taken from a session where Arthur talked about his loss of identity, his feeling of rejection and how this impacted on his not being able to learn: 'I just can't get anything inside my brain. I don't know who I am. My brother lives with my dad. My other brother knows where my father lives but they won't tell me. I want to see my father, talk to him, say, "Father, I am your son."'

I felt that Arthur wanted me to find the answer to his problems. He gave me the painful part of himself in the hope that I might find a cure. It felt as though I was being tested as to whether I could 'contain' this pain and make some sense of it for him, but it evoked extreme pain within me, a teacher attempting to work therapeutically. The impossibly excessive demands he made helped me to realise that psychotherapy might be a more appropriate intervention for Arthur. I felt his inability to hold on to any learning symbolised his deep sense of rejection and loss.

Martha

Martha lived with her mother, father and an older sister until her mother died when she was 16 years old. After the death she was sent to live with her elder sister for a few months before moving into a residential home. Some time later Martha's father married a woman who shares the same name as Martha's real mother. Martha's father now has a new family of three daughters, and Martha visits her father once a week. He phones her, arranges a date and collects her. She says that she always looks at her day centre and the college on her way to her father's to make sure the buildings have not been broken into. Martha never talked about her family or personal life during her class-time with me. While other students tended to chatter and needed reminding to concentrate on set tasks, Martha never voluntarily spoke to me in the lessons.

During classroom lessons Martha recoiled when I touched her as a way of praise, while other students responded favourably to this gesture. During the lessons Martha stared at me intensely. Her thick lenses, gaping mouth, and old-fashioned clothes created a non-attractive image that gave an appearance of 'low intelligence'. I was puzzled by her behaviour towards me while aware that she wanted something from me. When the opportunity to undertake educational therapy presented itself, I chose Martha. I sensed there was more to her than the 'mentally retarded' image. I felt threatened by her constant staring and sensed she was challenging me, but for what reason?

Martha had recoiled when I touched her as a way of praise. I reacted to this by finding reasons to spend less time with her while working with the more attractive, talkative students who visibly responded to my teaching methods. Martha worked quickly and was always the first to show me her work. I tried not to show my displeasure at her untidy, scored-out writing and her total lack of understanding of addition and subtraction signs. Her speed of work interfered with my time to think of ways to help the group understand their learning problems. I felt anxious and inadequate in my teaching and I knew that I had to make a fresh start. While I understood Martha's needs to improve her communication for learning, I realised that I would like her better if she could express herself other than by making grunting noises and staring at me. The need to stop Martha rushing herself, and me, required thinking about.

One-to-one with Martha

Martha agreed to work with me for one hour a week for 15 weeks. I explained the contract of turning up at a set time and suggested some areas of work. Over a period of three years, while teaching her basic numeracy, literacy and communication, I used my classroom observations of Martha to draw up a structure for our individual educational therapy sessions. I considered the main area of concern to be Martha's poor speech. This had reinforced the barrier between Martha and me for I could not know what Martha had grasped from my teaching. I moved between feelings of frustration and anger because I could not make sense of her monosyllabic replies or grunts which she gave as a means of response, while at the same time refusing to let me out of her sight.

My primary goal was to get Martha using simple sentences that made sense to her and her intended listener. In order to achieve this goal I used my art and drama teaching background as I felt this would lessen the anxiety for us both and also provide Martha with another vehicle of expression when words would not serve her purpose. By using simple instructions with pictorial representations and role playing I acknowledged that Martha was functioning at the concrete or symbolic stage of thinking. It became apparent during our sessions that Martha enjoyed repeating tasks where she could achieve with the bonus of being praised for her achievements. She became anxious when new tasks were introduced, such as subtraction (she had mastered addition). At an early stage of working together I was aware of this reluctance in her to accept change; I acknowledged her fear of change and its associations. Martha rarely spoke voluntarily.

Early educational therapy sessions with Martha soon revealed her attachment to her dead mother. I felt this loss was very great in view of her early stage of emotional development, although chronologically 24. She was unable to remember how old she was when her mother died, and she was confused when asked her age. Our time together gave Martha an opportunity to express her anger at her father for 'cheating' on her mother. She imagined the father was responsible for the mother's stroke which led to her death. I was surprised at the easy flow of her speech when recounting this information.

The problems relating to learning became more apparent when I started working therapeutically with Martha but I became more confident when thinking about the causes of her not being able to learn. I gradually realised that Martha's speed of work was connected with her desire to please and was her way of getting me to notice her. At the beginning of building a relationship with her she felt secure enough to take her time and appreciate that it was all right to get things wrong without losing my support.

Interactive processes used with Martha

When working with an adult who is cognitively and emotionally functioning at a lower level than their chronological age, it is difficult to find materials that are age-appropriate when skills and experiences are limited and coupled with a long history of institutions. She displayed the characteristics of learned helplessness in her deferential behaviour and in her inappropriate dress which was denying her womanhood. I assumed, too, that this had been exacerbated by her limited life-experiences commonly associated with people from residential homes.

First session

My first session alone with Martha made me anxious as she rushed the tasks I set her without understanding them. After a period of unease I decided to do what I felt most comfortable with, which was art. I used art as a means of breaking down tensions, both for myself and the student when we became 'stuck' in our learning. This provided a non-threatening atmosphere where we could feel free to work alone or together through a shared activity. During our time of silence I noticed Martha's eyes focus on the plain piece of paper, which I knew she associated with writing. I suggested that we might draw. Martha seized a piece of paper for herself. This action of 'doing' was Martha's way of dispelling awkward silences. I explained an exercise on drawing one another's hand. I did a drawing first and talked about the fingers joining. Martha repeated the exercise but voluntarily moved my hand into a position before drawing. I commented on Martha's good sense in getting things right and she looked pleased. This was the first time that Martha made contact with me and it felt like a tremendous step forward.

The atmosphere was now set for us to continue with this work so I decided to talk to Martha about the processes of drawing while holding her in focus. Martha's hand drawings showed fingers stuck on to hands (Figure 12.2). I held Martha's hand while tracing her fingers and hand and talked about joining together.

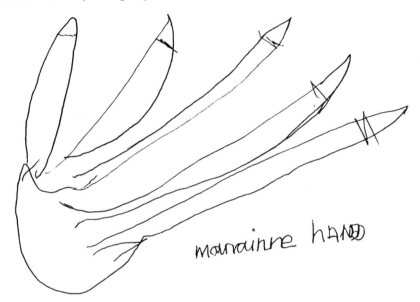

Mairaine hand

Figure 12.2 Martha's 'Hands'.

At the end of the session, I gave Martha five minutes of free choice while letting her know this is how we would work together each week. She chose to draw animals that reminded me of tadpoles (Figure 12.3). I felt this was a message concerning Martha's sexual experiences where she was unconsciously telling me something. These images were a recurring theme in the five drawings she religiously produced as voluntary homework. Some drawings acted as a channel of communication, where I sensed Martha wanted to tell me something she was struggling with (Figure 12.4). During the session I tried to bring this 'unknown thing' to the surface during our story-making but Martha cleverly evaded my attempts by changing the subject. Here is an example of how Martha did this:

M.S.   'I wondered if the girl bear is happy?'
A long silence followed this question which was broken by Martha coughing.
Martha   'Bad cough.'
I acknowledged her action by responding:
M.S.   'It sounds as if your cough is tickling your throat.'
Martha   'Bad cough.' (This was said with a smile.)

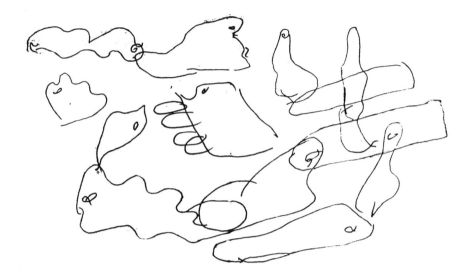

Figure 12.3 Martha's 'Tadpoles'.

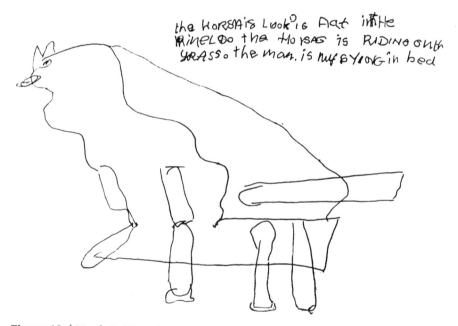

the HoRSA is Look⁰i 6 Aat iⁿ̄tte
ㅏⁱⁿⅇⱠⲈo the Hoʏsⅇ is RIDINo ouᵗ
ʏⱤㅏssₒ the maₙ. is ㅍㅼᵧᵢ₀ⱱᴳih bᵉd

Figure 12.4 Martha's 'Horse'.

I did not know where to take the story from here but sensed Martha
was telling me that she didn't want to continue. I remembered her interest in animals so decided to work on this. She quickly pushed a piece of
paper across for me to write down the animals she knew (cat, dog, cow).

When I asked how they might link together to make a story, she replied, 'Milk'. I considered this to be an interesting connection that might relate to the drawings of tadpoles and her fear of being touched.

Martha continued to produce voluntary homework images, and during the eleventh session she showed me a page of outlined and coloured numbers, and an 'alphabet' which contained the word 'rod'. I drew this to Martha's attention. She replied, 'Volunteer. Says he loves me. Don't tell anyone. Get sack.' I was initially filled with a sense of relief as, at last, Martha had trusted me enough to let me know her secret. I let Martha know that I sensed she wanted to tell me something but she needed time. This revelation made me feel proud of Martha's bravery and showed it by thanking her for trusting me with her secret.

Martha did not produce drawings of tadpoles any more. I was to find out much later that Bob was a voluntary worker at Martha's previous Day Centre who had sexual intercourse with Martha without her consent. Since this revelation her artwork became decorative with a greater amount of detail. She joined an art class and was more aware of what the other students were doing. She became ambitious to produce realistic images. This was an enormous step forward for her as she was now able to think about life outside herself. There has been a noticeable development in Martha's ability to make herself understood to myself and others. The insight gained while applying an educational therapy approach enabled me to examine events that could have prevented learning while working with Martha on our common goals.

Clay as an aid to concrete thinking

As Martha was not able to work on tasks involving abstract thought, I realised that I must start with her concrete thinking skills. Working with clay was introduced as a way of exploring shapes in their 3D form (shapes are part of the Mathematics syllabus). As well as using clay to understand shapes, I wanted Martha to experience the sensation of touching, in a positive sense, for creative purposes, but also as a different means of communicating, i.e., through symbolic language.

I introduced Martha's family into the session by suggesting that she build a house like her father's. I talked about the shapes of windows, doors and the roof on a worksheet. Martha had to make these shapes while identifying them. She found difficulty in associating the clay shape with the one on the worksheet. I did a drawing of a house based on Martha's description, intending to give her a starting point or means of reference. Instead of using the drawing to build her own house she proceeded to stick shapes on top of the drawing. This action irritated me as she had not grasped the instruction but perhaps I was not taking the time to check her understanding.

My intention was to help Martha think about her family and especially her father, whom she seldom mentioned. She needed help fitting the pieces relating to her mother dying and her part in it. I felt that by building a clay house Martha might be able to work through her painful thoughts while I was there with her. I sensed her anger and resentment at having to continue the exercise of building a house. She revealed her feelings through roughly pulling pieces of clay and placing them on the drawing without any regard for the image being created. I felt frustrated and annoyed at her failure to appreciate a simple instruction. On reflection, I saw this to be the reaction of a didactic teacher rather than the adoption of the therapeutic approach that I was learning about in the diploma course.

Martha tried to make the clay house stand but it fell apart. I commented that life can be like that and sometimes things do not work for me. I suggested that the house needed a back, but Martha turned her head away from me without speaking. I then suggested that Martha might like to make a family. The following dialogue took place.

Martha 'Didn't see your car this morning.'

(Since starting our educational therapy sessions, Martha has begun recounting the days and places she saw my car as she passed the college on her way to the day centre. This seemed to be an example of her growing attachment to me. I felt that she did not want to dwell on her family, and she was stopping me from taking it further by changing the subject.)

Martha (continues) 'What do you do on Fridays?'
M.S.   'Oh, you are wondering why I don't have students on Friday. I write letters, and use the phone and I work with you on Fridays.'
Martha 'I will see you Monday.' (Martha attends college on a Tuesday. Here she is referring to seeing my car.)

I felt that Martha needed reassuring that she was my special student on Fridays. I talked about how we met on Fridays to help her with education and improve her talking skills. She appeared pleased with herself. Martha continued making a clay person while we talked and said, 'It looks like you.' When I put the statement back to Martha, 'Like me?', she told me she was doing it differently. When I tried to expand on this, Martha replied, 'Don't know'.

Martha worked quietly while making clay figures, but occasionally gave me an account of personal details. She talked about her father phoning, but when I asked how she felt when he phoned, she replied, 'Can't remember'. Later she complained that she was 'cheesed off with Fridays'. Then she said how she liked Fridays with me. I said I enjoyed our time together. Martha talked about her bad stomach, attributing this to 'women's problems'. I found this personal remark embarrassing and difficult to handle, possibly because it was unexpected.

When Martha did not want to continue with a topic she demonstrated this by working quicker and roughly pulling strips of clay without regard for the subject. I felt she needed space to act out her 'bad' side while easing her back to being 'in control' of herself. Martha was unable to say how old she was, and what age she was when her mother died. When we talked about this, she replied, 'Don't know', and then changed the subject (e.g., 'It's raining outside'). I found this response difficult to deal with and allowed Martha to control the ending. Perhaps by reminding Martha of pleasurable associations with her mother, such as family holidays at the seaside, it would help her to hold on to the good times in her past life.

I had introduced clay to help Martha overcome her anxiety regarding touching, but to maintain an educational input we continued with shapes. This time we also used our bodies to explore the sensations of touching. This took the form of using our fingers to trace our own bodies while I talked about the flat areas, and the fact that we had a back and sides. I felt this related to Martha's one-dimensional drawings of animals and outlined people. Martha laughed but appeared slightly embarrassed when we touched.

Conversation related to a drawing session

Martha did most of her unprompted talking during the drawing time. For example, she started telling me about her sister and how she took Martha to the pub. I took this opportunity to find out Martha's age when her mother died by asking how old her sister was at that time. Martha responded, 'Don't remember how old I was when Mum died.' This idea of replacing another person with herself was a frequent occurrence during the early sessions; for example:

M.S.   'How many children are there in your father's family?'
Martha   'I've got Jo, Joanne, Joylene.'

A later example of how Martha felt comfortable enough to give me a private insight to her past through her drawing was when she drew a man during her free-choice time in session seven.

M.S.   'Does that man remind you of anyone?'
Martha   'Bob. Other day centre.'

Martha talked about how her father had told lies to her mother. She blamed him for cheating on her mother and said that it caused her mother to die of a stroke. I was taken aback by the lucidity of Martha's flow of speech while relating this part of her life to me, which was in marked contrast to her usual way of communicating. I felt that this was a rare moment for Martha to show her anger and share a family secret. Did Martha feel safe to open herself to me because I was not asking her questions? Had I prepared the way for her through showing that I was an emotionally available person for her? This major step forward in our learning and understanding together made me question if Martha used her poor speech as a protection from intrusive comments by others. Her ability to speak lucidly and with passion revealed someone who felt deeply. People like Martha are supposed to be 'no trouble' to anyone. I often feel they are not supposed to get angry.

My own problems of understanding

Through applying educational therapy techniques I hoped to gain an understanding of the blocks in Martha's learning, as well as giving her space to talk about herself. As I was not given an assessment record of her level of functioning when she arrived, I started from evidence I had gained during class time. Martha never talked about her family, or if she did, I never understood her. As most students enjoy talking about themselves, I imagined that Martha would too. This assumption proved wrong as she bluntly ignored my attempts to draw her out. Working with her individually I had the additional problem of developing her speech while understanding her avoidance of letting me know her.

For three years in the classroom I had not understood what Martha was saying. She sat far away from me and responded to questions with grunting or mumbling sounds. I invested considerable time in developing the students' communication skills, and I was annoyed at Martha's apparently uncooperative attitude. I had success with other students through role-playing exercises during drama sessions, but Martha made me feel incompetent as a teacher because she did not give me the responses I wanted.

Martha's constant vigilance made her different from the beginning. As I mentioned before, her intense staring unnerved me. This behaviour, coupled with her 'special needs' look of gaping mouth, I realised, was distasteful to me, although I wanted to bring Martha into the group.

Martha's speech was an area in which I felt inadequate, because I was not convinced that formal methods of teaching phonetics would help. However, she needed to make herself understood not only to me but to others with whom she had daily contact. I realised early in the sessions that Martha wanted to be 'doing'. She saw writing as working. Once during an awkward silence I wondered aloud about drawing as another way of communicating. This was to be our escape valve at every awkward situation. I felt that it rescued me in times of 'not knowing' as much as Martha. Drawing provided the means of reuniting us when I did not know the answer and Martha did not want to tell me.

Martha's inability to accept touching as a means of praise caused me concern after my initial annoyance at her further rebuking me. I saw the link in her constant vigilance of me and her recoiling when I went near her, but I could not make sense of it. It was only later in our individual sessions that I was able to learn of Martha's sexual abuse at the hands of a much older man. In our earlier sessions Martha gave me clues through symbols, e.g. animal drawings (see Figures 12.3 and 12.4), which I did not immediately recognise, but I let her know that I knew that she had a secret. I found it hard to wait for this to be revealed as this contrasted with her constantly 'rushing' me in other areas.

During a part of our programme on time I discovered that Martha was giving mixed messages. When asked whether she knew the time, she always replied 'No.' She then completed a sheet on the hour, half-hour and quarter-hour, correctly. This puzzled me as her residential home had voiced concern over Martha's time-keeping being always too early. I linked this with Martha not knowing her age and yet she could remember college appointments and incidents related to college with complete accuracy. This set me wondering about the connection between Martha saying she didn't know the time, or her age or the time of her mother's death, and Martha's apparent attachment to me.

I imagined Martha's reserved nature prevented her from expressing her feelings or asking questions relating to the death of her mother. Through providing Martha with space to feel, I hoped I had helped her manage painful thoughts. Was Martha's constant rushing related to her wanting to learn? Or to please me? Or to block out painful thoughts? By acknowledging the painful areas of Martha's life I was showing her that it was all right to express one's feelings without being disloyal or losing chosen people's affections. By providing a secure environment where Martha could begin to communicate her frightening thoughts she might make sense of her mother's death and her perceived part in it.

My own Learning

I referred earlier to boundaries. My educational therapy sessions took place in the room where I taught my other students and Martha: the only obvious difference being the shoe box containing her special materials for the sessions. This simple feature was enough to transform the setting while allowing us to take on our other roles.

While working with Arthur I felt overwhelmed by his sadness when he talked about not knowing who he was and his family rejection. I felt unable to contain his grief as I was inexperienced at giving it back to him in a manageable form.

My frustrations lay in trying to understand the causes of sadness, and his were manifested in disruptive/rude behaviour. While feeling unable to make everything right for him, I realised that I needed to manage my own feelings in order to continue my attempts to teach my other students in a therapeutic manner.

Unlike Arthur, who bombarded me with his life story, I needed to work hard at enabling Martha to talk about aspects of her life that I felt were troubling her. She felt secure enough to talk about personal matters such as death, sexual abuse and her periods, and realised that she was taking it upon herself to behave in an adult way. I continued to have difficulty in being able to adjust to Martha's young level of intellectual performance while keeping in mind her more adult emotional and physical level of functioning.

Pressure to learn creates anxiety both for the teacher and the student. I found it difficult not to transfer this pressure on to the educational therapy sessions. It was important to remind myself that the focus was on the process and not on rushing to achieve an end product. The group supervision I received, coupled with practice, went some way to maintaining my dual roles. It has provided me with the strength to continue teaching in a manner that acknowledges the impact of the students' well-being on their learning.

Conclusion

I have examined my experience while applying an educational therapy approach with adults who displayed a range of disabilities and in the process focused on:

- The effects of a long-term insecure base (anxious attachment);
- The benefits of providing a secure teaching base to enable learning to take place;
- The connection between emotional and cognitive performance;
- Art materials as a way of communicating.

If one can provide a facilitating environment (Winnicott, 1965), both adult and pupil can learn. Barrett and Trevitt (1991) wrote about the role of an 'educational attachment figure' while emphasising the need to maintain professional boundaries. (I agree, some of my students have called me 'Mummy'.) The intention of the therapist is to 'hold on' to painful memories, thus freeing the learner to nourish intellectual and emotional needs. I advocate that by enabling the students to express their painful thoughts and memories through the use of educational therapy techniques, they can place such thoughts in a context, and free a space in their minds for developing cognitive skills.

The technique of recording, evaluating and planning the sessions enabled me to make what seemed an almost unmanageable task manageable.

Conclusion

The study carried out with Martha revealed my prejudices against an outwardly unattractive student who appeared withdrawn. Through spending time with her I discovered someone who could learn practical tasks such as using a calculator and basic word-processing skills. Martha has completed her English Level One, a nationally recognised qualification. Her presentation on paper is no longer scored over many times. Her persistence has been rewarded as she is learning to travel using public transport, and is attending evening classes. Practical suggestions on my visits to Martha's residence resulted in a new hairstyle, fashionable shoes/clothes and a watch. These, I feel, are examples of how one area of growth can nourish another. I have valued the experience of time spent investigating and acknowledging the painful thoughts of both student and teacher.

Bibliography

Abrahamsen G (1983) 'Jeg-psykologi, klinisk pedagogikk og A.M.S.-metoden. En vurdering av A.M.S.-metoden som en barne-psykiatrisk pedagogisk observasjonsmetode' ('An appraisal of the A.M.S. method as an observation method in child psychiatry'). Hovedoppgave ved Universitetet i Trondheim, Norges Lærerhøgskole. MA thesis, University of Trondheim.

Ainsworth MDS (1967) Infancy in Uganda: Infant Care and the Growth of Attachment. Baltimore: John Hopkins University Press.

Ainsworth MDS, Wittig BA (1969) 'Attachment and explanatory behaviour of one-year-olds in a strange situation' in Foss BW (ed) Determinants of Infant Behaviour IV. London: Methuen.

Allen P (1986) Herbert & Harry. London: Hamish Hamilton.

Alvarez A (1994) Live Company. London, New York: Tavistock and Routledge.

Barrett M, Trevitt J (1991) Attachment Behaviour and the School Child – an Introduction to Educational Therapy. London, New York: Routledge.

—(1994) 'Consultation to a school subsystems by a teacher' in Dowling E, Osborne E (eds) The Family and the School. London, New York: Routledge.

Barrows K (1984) 'A child's difficulties in using his gifts and his imagination.' Journal of Child Psychotherapy vol.10, no.1.

Beaumont M (1988) 'The effect of loss on learning: the stillborn sibling.' Journal of Educational Therapy vol.2, no.1.

—(1991) 'Reading between the lines; the child's fear of meaning.' Journal of Psychoanalytic Psychotherapy vol.5, no.3.

Bender LA (1938) 'A visual motor Gestalt test and its clinical use.' American Orthopsychiatric Association Research Monographs: No.3 in Anastasi A (1982) Psychological Testing 5th edn. New York, London: Macmillan.

Bernstein PP, Duncan SW, Gavin LA, Lindahl KM, Ozonoff S (1989) 'Resistance to psychotherapy after a child dies: the effect of the death on parents and siblings.' Psychotherapy Today vol.26, University of Denver, Colorado.

Bettelheim B, Zelan K (1982) On Learning to Read: the Child's Fascination with Meaning. London: Thames & Hudson.

—(1987) A Good Enough Parent. London: Thames & Hudson.

Bion WR (1962a) Learning from Experience. London: Heinemann.

—(1962b) 'A theory of thinking.' International Journal of Psychoanalysis XLIII, pp. 4 and 5.

Bjerknes Tolsa E (1982) 'Fra barneskole til ungdomsskole. En longitudinell pedgogisk studie med A.M.S.-metode, T.M.T.og B.G.T. av barn i 2. og 8. klasse' ('From primary school to secondary school – a longitudinal study by use of the A.M.S.

method'), Hovedoppgave ved Statens Spesiallærerhøgskole. MA thesis, University of Oslo.

Blanchard P (1946) 'Psychoanalytic contributions to the problems of reading.' The Psychoanalytic Study of the Child vol. 2.

Bo-Ege (1985) Sprogtest I. Danmark Spesialpedagogiske forlag.

Bowlby J (1969) 'Attachment' in Attachment and Loss 1. London: Hogarth Press and Institute of Psychoanalysis, New York: Basic Books.

—(1973) 'Separation: anxiety and anger' in Attachment and Loss 2. London: Hogarth Press and Institute of Psychoanalysis; New York: Basic Books.

—(1979) 'On Knowing what you are not supposed to know and feeling what you are not supposed to feel.' Canadian Journal of Psychiatry 24: 403–8.

—(1980) 'Loss, sadness and depression' in Attachment and Loss 3. London: Hogarth Press and Institute of Psychoanalysis; New York: Basic Books.

—(1982) 'Attachment and loss: retrospect and prospect.' American Journal of Orthopsychiatry 52.

—(1988) A Secure Base: Clinical Applications of Attachment Theory. London: Routledge.

Britton R, Feldman M, O'Shaughnessy E (1989) in Steiner J (ed) The Oedipus Complex Today, Clinical Implications. London: Karnac Books.

Brown DG (1992) 'Bion and Foulkes: basic assumptions and beyond' in Pines M (ed) Bion and Group Psychotherapy. London: Routledge.

Caplan G (1970) The Theory and Practice of Mental Health Consultation. London: Tavistock.

Case C (1990) Images of Art Therapy – New Developments in Theory and Practice. London, New York: Routledge.

—(1994) 'Art therapy in analysis – advance/retreat in the belly of the spider' in Inscape vol.1 pp. 5–10, Journal of the British Association of Art Therapy.

Caspari I (1974) 'Educational therapy' in Varma V (ed) Psychotherapy Today. London: Constable.

—(1976) Troublesome Children in Class. London: Routledge & Kegan Paul.

Chitty S (1971) The Woman Who Wrote Black Beauty: A Life of Anna Sewell. London: Hodder & Stoughton.

Cockett M, Tripp J (1994) The Exeter Family Study – Family Breakdown and its Impact on Children. Exeter: University of Exeter Press.

Copley B, Forryan B (1987) Therapeutic work with Children and Young People. London: Robert Royce.

Croll P, Moses D (1985) One in Five – the Assessment and Incidence of Special Educational Needs. London: Routledge & Kegan Paul.

Dahl R (1970) Fantastic Mr Fox. London: Puffin Books.

—(1971) The Minpins. London: Jonathan Cape.

Dale F (1992) in The Management of Children with Emotional and Behaviour Disorders in Varma V (ed). London: Fulton.

Department of Education (1982) Educational Statistics in Schools. London: HMSO.

Dockar-Drysdale B(1993) Therapy and Consultation in Child Care. London: Free Association Books.

Dowling E, Osborne E (1985, 2nd edn 1994) The Family and the School – A Joint System Approach to Working with Children. London: Routledge & Kegan Paul.

Drake A (1991) 'Truants from Life' in Varma V (ed). London: Fulton.

Duve A-M (1965) 'Om psykodynamikk og læring'. ('Psychodynamics and Learning'). Oslo: Stensil. pp. 2, 3, 63.

—(1974) 'A.M.S.-testen. En barnepsykiatrisk pedagogisk observasjon'. ('The A.M.S. test: an educational assessment method'). Oslo: Stensil. p.13.

—(1988) 'The Norwegian Educational Assessment Method.' Journal of Educational Therapy vol.2, no.1.

Elton Report (1989) Discipline in Schools: Report of the Committee of enquiry into Discipline in Schools. London: HMSO.

Fossen A, Diseth TH (1991) Kortidsterapi med barn (Short-term therapy with children). Oslo: Universitetsforlaget.

Foulkes SH, Anthony EJ (1984) Group Psychotherapy: The Psychoanalytic Approach. London: Marefield Reprints.

Freud A (1965) Normality and Pathology in Childhood, 7th Printing. New York: International Universities Press.

Freud S (1926) Inhibitions, Symptoms and Anxiety, standard edition vol.XX. London: Hogarth Press.

—(1931) Female Sexuality, standard edition, vol. XXI. London: Hogarth Press.

Galloway P (1985) Schools, Pupils and Special Educational Needs. London: Croom Helm.

Geddes H (1991) 'An evaluation of teacher support groups', MA dissertation, University of Surrey.

Goodenough F (1926) Measurement of Intelligence by Drawings. New York: Harcourt Brace & World.

Greenhalgh P(1986) 'Holding explorations', Educational Therapy Journal no.5.

—(1994)Emotional Growth and Learning. London, New York: Routledge.

Hanko G (1985, 1990) Special Needs in Ordinary Classrooms. London: Blackwell.

High H (1978) 'Processes in educational therapy' FAET Supplement no.11.

—(1985) 'The use of indirect communication in educational therapy.' Journal of Educational Therapy vol.1, no.1.

Holdhus V (1987) 'Klinisk pedagogikk. Et forsøk på å beskrive klinisk pedagogisk behandling slik den er utviklet ved Nic Waals Institut'. Hovedopggave ved Universitetet i Oslo. (Educational therapy described as it has been developed at Nic Waals Institute. MA thesis, University of Oslo.)

Hughes T (1968) The Iron Man. London: Faber & Faber.

Jungmann A, Axeworthy A (1987) I Don't Want to go to School. London: Heinemann.

Klein M (1931) The Theory of Intellectual Inhibitions. London: Hogarth Press.

—(1946) 'Notes on some schizoid mechanism' in Development in Psychoanalysis. London: Hogarth Press and The Institute of Psychoanalysis (1952).

—(1957) Envy and Gratitude. London: Hogarth Press.

Kolvin I, Garside RS, Nicol AR, MacMillan A, Wolstenhome F, Leitch IM (1981) Help Starts Here. London: Tavistock.

Kübler-Ross K (1983) On Children and Death. London: Macmillan.

La Trobe (1991) Twins in School. La Trobe twin study. Dept. of Psychology, Melbourne University, Australia. Melbourne: Multiple Birth Association.

Lewin K (1935) 'Education for reality' selected papers, Chap.5 in A Dynamic Theory of Personality. New York, London: McGraw-Hill.

Linnesch D Greenspoon (1988) Adolescent Art Therapy. New York: Brunner-Mazel. p.142.

Marstrander A (1991) 'Hva kan barns atferd fortelle? AMS-metoden til bruk i en klinisk småbarnspedagogisk observasjon av barn med sykdommen leddgikt' ('What can the attitude of children tell us by use of the AMS method?'). Hovedoppgave ved Universitetet i Oslo, Institutt for spesial-pedagogikk. MA thesis, University of Oslo.

McMahon L (1992) The Handbook of Play Therapy. London: Routledge.

Milner M (1955) 'The role of illusion in symbol formation' in Klein M et al., (eds) New Directions in Psychoanalysis. London: Tavistock.

Mossige S (1993) 'Metafor som en terapeutisk intervensjon' ('Metaphor as a therapeutic intervention). Artikkel fra forelesning. Lecture at Ullevaal Hospital, Oslo.

Murray L (1991a) 'Inter-subjectivity, object relations theory and empirical evidence from mother–infant interaction'. Special Issue: 'The Effects of Relationships on Relationships.' Infant Mental Health Journal vol. 12. pp.219–232.

—(1991b) 'Infant Roots of Infant Cognition in Early Relationships: A Prospective Study of the Impact of Maternal Depression on Infant Cognitive Development.' Infant Mental Health Journal vol. 12.

Newton M, Thomson M (1982) Aston Index (Revised). Cambridge: Living and Learning.

Obholzer A (1992) The Secret Life of Vulnerable Children, in Varma V (ed). London: Routledge.

Oram H (1984) Angry Arthur. London: Andersen.

Orbach S (1993) in The Guardian newspaper (13 November).

Osborne E, Barrett M (1985) in Dowling E, Osborne E (eds) (1st edn 1985) The Family and the School: a Joint Systems Approach to Problems with Children. London: Routledge & Kegan Paul.

Pedagogisk-psykologisk ordbok.(1984) Oslo: Kunnskapsforlaget.

Piontelli A(1989) 'A study on twins before and after birth.' International Review of Psychoanalysis.

Pollock G (1986) 'Childhood sibling loss: a family tragedy.' Psychiatric Annals vol. 16, part 5, pp. 309–14.

Pratt J (1978) 'Perceived stress among teachers.' Educational Review 30.

Racker H (1968) Transference and Counter-Transference. New York: International Universities Press.

Rando TA (1985) 'Resistance to creating therapeutic rituals in the psychotherapy of the bereaved.' Psychotherapy vol.22, no.2, pp.236–240. University of Denver, Colorado.

Rosen H (1986) 'When a sibling dies.' International Journal of Family Psychiatry vol.17, p.4.

Ross T (1987) Oscar got the Blame. London: Beaver.

Rourke BP, Feurst DR (1991) Learning Disabilities and Psychological Functioning. New York: Guilford Press.

Rutter M (1975) Helping Troubled Children. London: Penguin.

Rye H (1993) Tidlig hjelp til bedre samspill (Early help to a better communication). Oslo: Universitetsforlaget. pp.22, 23 and 64.

Segal H (1957) 'Notes on symbol formation.' International Journal of Psychoanalysis vol. 38, p.1.

Schaffer R (1990) 'Early social development' in Woodhead M, Carr R, Light P (eds) Becoming a Person: Child Development in a Social Context vol. 1. London: Routledge and Open University.

Spinetta JJ, Spinetta P (1981) Living with Childhood Cancer. St. Louis: C.V. Mosby.

Steig W (1972) Amos and Boris. London: Hamish Hamilton.

Stern D (1985) The Interpersonal World of the Infant. London: Basic Books.

Trower P, Bryant B, Argyle M, (1978) Social Skills and Mental Health. London: Methuen.

Varley S (1984) Badger's Parting Gifts. London: Andersen Press.

Vipont E, Briggs R (1971) The Elephant and the Bad Baby. London: Picture Puffin.

Warnock M (1978) Special Educational Needs: the Report of the Committee of

Inquiry into the Education of Handicapped Children and Young People – The Warnock Report. London: HMSO.

Winnicott DW (1965) The Maturational Processes and the Facilitating Environment. London: Hogarth Press; Toronto: Clarke Irwin.

—(1971) Playing and Reality. London: Tavistock.

—(1986) (pub. posthumously) Home is Where We Start From. London: WW Norton.

Ystgaard M (1993) 'Sårbar ungdom og sosial støtte' ('Vulnerable youth and social support'). Oslo: Senter for sosialt nettverk og helse. Rapport nr. 1.

Index